CONTENTS

Introduction

You will find plenty in these pages to inspire you: cold, light soups to refresh your palate on a hot summer's day; rich and creamy soups to slide like velvet over your taste buds; spicy soups to warm and comfort you on a cold winter's day; and hearty soups, full of goodness, to provide a satisfying lunch when hunger strikes. Here, in one collection, are soups for any occasion.

Few dishes give more all-round pleasure than a good home made soup, so it is hardly surprising that some soups feature in every cuisine around the world – as readers of this book will discover – whether they are called gumbos, potages, broths, chowders or consommés. Now that once-unfamiliar ingredients are readily available in specialist food shops and many supermarkets, the world of soups is yours to explore.

Good soup is easy to make, especially if you take care to choose the freshest ingredients, including those in season. A good stock is necessary as the basis for many – though by no means all – soups. This takes time to make, but large quantities of stock can be prepared in advance and frozen in smaller portions to await a bout of soup making at your convenience. Recipes for basic vegetable, fish, meat, poultry, Chinese and Japanese stocks are given in the following pages.

The right garnish, too, enhances even the simplest soup; giving careful thought to the presentation of your soup adds a professional finish. Herby croûtons or crunchy leek haystacks, for example, arranged in the centre of your soup adds a contrasting texture and a complementary flavour. A swirl of cream or a sprinkling of fresh herbs enhances any dish. Try out the suggested garnishes, then have fun developing your own perfect finishes.

Each soup recipe in this collection features step-by-step instructions, many of them illustrated, to guide you through the entire soup-making process. Beautiful colour pictures show the finished dish – which means that even the most intricate soup is within your reach. So take your time to try out many of the delicious and nutritious recipes featured here. You will soon grow in confidence and begin to change the basic recipes here and there to create your own personalized favourites.

Whether you have yet to discover the satisfaction gained from making and eating your own soup at home, or are an experienced soup maker who wants to increase your repertoire of recipes, you need look no further than the pages of this beautifully-illustrated book for inspiration. Turn the page and savour the recipes.

Making Your Own Stocks

Fresh stocks are indispensable for creating good home-made soups. They add a depth of flavour that plain water just cannot achieve.

Although many supermarkets now sell tubs of fresh stock, these can work out expensive, especially if you need large quantities for your cooking. Making your own is surprisingly easy and much more economical, particularly if you can use leftovers – the chicken carcass from Sunday lunch, for example, or the shells you're left with once you've peeled prawns (shrimp). But home-made stocks aren't just cheaper, they're also tastier and much more nutritious, precisely because they're made with fresh, natural ingredients.

You can, of course, use stock (bouillon) cubes or granules, but be sure to check the seasoning, as these tend to be high in salt.

One good idea for keen and regular soup makers is to freeze home-made stock in plastic freezer bags, or ice cube trays, so you always have a supply at your disposal whenever you need some.

Frozen stock can be stored in the freezer for up to six months. Make sure that you label each stock carefully for easy identification.

Use the appropriate stock for the soup you are making. Onion soup, for example, is improved with a good beef stock. Be particularly careful to use a vegetable stock if you are catering for vegetarians.

Recipes are given on the following pages for vegetable stock, chicken stock, meat stock, fish stock and basic stocks for Chinese and Japanese soups.

Vegetable Stock

Use this versatile stock as the basis for all vegetarian soups.

INGREDIENTS

Makes 2.5 litres/4½ pints/11 cups

2 leeks, coarsely chopped
3 celery sticks, coarsely chopped
1 large onion, unpeeled, chopped
2 pieces fresh root ginger, chopped
1 yellow (bell) pepper, seeded
  and chopped
1 parsnip, chopped
mushroom stalks
tomato peelings
45ml/3 tbsp light soy sauce
3 bay leaves
bunch of parsley stalks
3 fresh thyme sprigs
1 fresh rosemary sprig
10ml/2 tsp salt
freshly ground black pepper
3.5 litres/6 pints/15 cups water

1 Put all the ingredients into a very large pan. Gradually bring to the boil, then lower the heat and simmer for 30 minutes, stirring occasionally.

2 Leave to cool. Strain, then discard the vegetables. The stock is ready to use. Alternatively, chill or freeze the stock and keep it to use as required.

Index

Fish Stock

Fish stock is much quicker to make than poultry or meat stock. Ask your fishmonger for heads, bones and trimmings from white fish.

Makes about 1 litre/1³/₄ pints/4 cups

675g/1¹/₂lb heads, bones and trimmings
  from white fish

1 onion, sliced

2 celery sticks with leaves, chopped

1 carrot, sliced

¹/₂ lemon, sliced (optional)

1 bay leaf

a few fresh parsley sprigs

6 black peppercorns

1.35 litres/2¹/₄ pints/6 cups cold water

150ml/¹/₄ pint/²/₃ cup dry white wine

1 Rinse the fish heads, bones and trimmings well under cold running water. Put in a stockpot with the vegetables and lemon, if using, the herbs, peppercorns, water and wine. Bring to the boil, skimming the surface frequently, then reduce the heat and simmer for 25 minutes.

2 Strain the stock without pressing down on the ingredients in the sieve. If not using immediately, leave to cool and then store in the refrigerator. Fish stock should be used within 2 days, or it can be frozen for up to 3 months.

Beef Broth with Cassava

This "big" soup is almost like a stew. The addition of wine is not traditional, but enhances the richness of the broth.

INGREDIENTS

Serves 4

450 g/1 lb stewing beef, cubed

1.2 litres/2 pints/5 cups beef stock

300 ml/½ pint/1¼ cups white wine

15 ml/1 tbsp soft brown sugar

1 onion, finely chopped

1 bay leaf

1 bouquet garni

1 sprig of fresh thyme

15 ml/1 tbsp tomato purée

1 large carrot, sliced

275 g/10 oz cassava or yam, cubed

50 g/2 oz spinach, chopped

a little hot pepper sauce, to taste

salt and freshly ground black pepper

2 Add the carrot, cassava or yam, spinach, a few drops of hot pepper sauce, salt and pepper, and simmer for a further 15 minutes until both the meat and vegetables are tender. Serve.

1 Put the beef, stock, wine, sugar, onion, bay leaf, bouquet garni, thyme and tomato purée in a large saucepan, bring to the boil and then cover and simmer for about 1¼ hours.

> ### COOK'S TIP
>
> If you like, a cheap cut of lamb can be used instead of beef, and any other root vegetable can be used instead of, or as well as, the cassava or yam. Noodles, pasta shapes or macaroni can also be used as a base, in which case you can cut down on the root vegetables. You can, if you prefer, omit the wine and add more water.

Chicken Stock

A good home-made poultry stock is invaluable in the kitchen. If poultry giblets are available, add them (except the livers) with the wings. Once made, chicken stock can be kept in an airtight container in the refrigerator for 3–4 days, or frozen for up to 6 months.

INGREDIENTS

Makes about 2.5 litres/4 ¹/₂ pints/11 cups

1.2–1.5kg/2¹/₂–3lb chicken or turkey
(wings, backs and necks)

2 onions, unpeeled, quartered

1 tbsp olive oil

4 litres/7 pints/17¹/₂ cups cold water

2 carrots, coarsely chopped

2 celery sticks, with leaves if possible,
coarsely chopped

small handful of fresh parsley

few fresh thyme sprigs or
3.5ml/³/₄ tsp dried thyme

1 or 2 bay leaves

10 black peppercorns, lightly crushed

1 Combine the poultry wings, backs and necks in a stockpot with the onion quarters and the oil. Cook over a moderate heat, stirring occasionally, until the poultry and onions are lightly and evenly browned.

2 Add the water and stir well to mix in the sediment on the base of the pan. Bring to the boil and skim off the impurities as they rise to the surface of the stock.

3 Add the chopped carrots and celery, fresh parsley, thyme, bay leaf and black peppercorns. Partly cover the stockpot and gently simmer the stock for about 3 hours.

4 Strain the stock through a sieve into a bowl and leave to cool, then chill in the refrigerator for an hour.

5 When cold, carefully remove the layer of fat that will have set on the surface. Store in the refrigerator for 3–4 days or freeze until required.

Ginger, Chicken and Coconut Soup

This aromatic soup is rich with coconut milk and intensely flavoured with galangal, lemon grass and kaffir lime leaves.

INGREDIENTS

Serves 4–6

750ml/1¼ pints/3 cups coconut milk

475ml/16fl oz/2 cups Chicken Stock

4 lemon grass stalks, bruised and chopped

2.5cm/1in piece galangal, thinly sliced

10 black peppercorns, crushed

10 kaffir lime leaves, torn

300g/11oz skinless boneless chicken, cut into thin strips

115g/4oz button (white) mushrooms

50g/2oz/½ cup baby corn cobs

60ml/4 tbsp lime juice

45ml/3 tbsp Thai fish sauce

For the garnish

2 red chillies, seeded and chopped

3–4 spring onions (scallions), chopped

chopped fresh coriander (cilantro)

1 Bring the coconut milk and chicken stock to the boil in a large pan. Add the lemon grass, galangal, peppercorns and half the kaffir lime leaves, reduce the heat and simmer gently for 10 minutes.

2 Strain the stock mixture into a clean pan. Return to the heat, then add the chicken strips, mushrooms and baby corn cobs. Cook for about 5–7 minutes, until the chicken is cooked.

3 Stir in the lime juice, fish sauce to taste and the rest of the lime leaves. Ladle the soup into warm bowls, garnish with red chillies, spring onions and coriander and serve.

Meat Stock

The most delicious meat soups rely on a good home-made stock for success. Once it is made, meat stock can be kept in the refrigerator for 4–5 days, or frozen for longer storage (up to 6 months).

INGREDIENTS

Makes about 2 litres/3½ pints/9 cups

1.75kg/4lb beef bones, such as shin (shank), leg, neck and clod (chuck), or veal or lamb bones, cut into 6cm/2½in pieces

2 onions, unpeeled, quartered

2 carrots, coarsely chopped

2 celery sticks, with leaves if possible, coarsely chopped

2 tomatoes, coarsely chopped

4.5 litres/7½ pints/20 cups water

handful of parsley stalks

few fresh thyme sprigs or 3.5ml/¾ tsp dried thyme

2 bay leaves

10 black peppercorns, lightly crushed

1 Preheat the oven to 230°C/450°F/Gas 8. Put the bones in a roasting pan and roast, turning occasionally, for 30 minutes, until they start to brown.

2 Add the onions, carrots, celery and tomatoes and baste with the fat in the roasting pan. Return the pan to the oven and roast for a further 20–30 minutes, until the bones are well browned. Stir and baste occasionally.

3 Transfer the bones and roasted vegetables to a stockpot. Spoon off the fat from the roasting pan. Add a little of the water to the roasting pan and bring to the boil on the hob (stovetop), stirring well to scrape up any browned sediment. Pour this liquid into the stockpot.

4 Add the remaining water to the pot. Bring just to the boil, skimming frequently to remove all the foam from the surface. Add the parsley, thyme, bay leaves and black peppercorns.

5 Partly cover the stockpot and gently simmer the stock for 4–6 hours. All the bones and vegetables should always be covered with liquid, so top up with a little boiling water from time to time if necessary.

6 Strain the stock through a colander into a bowl, then skim as much fat as possible from the surface. If possible, cool the stock and then chill it in the refrigerator; the fat will rise to the top and set in a layer that can be removed easily.

Pork and Pickled Mustard Greens Soup

This highly flavoured soup makes an interesting start to a meal.

INGREDIENTS

Serves 4–6

225g/8oz pickled mustard leaves, soaked

50g/2oz cellophane noodles, soaked

15ml/1 tbsp vegetable oil

4 garlic cloves, thinly sliced

1 litre/1¾ pints/4 cups Chicken Stock

450g/1lb pork ribs, cut into large chunks

30ml/2 tbsp Thai fish sauce

pinch of sugar

ground black pepper

2 fresh red chillies, seeded and thinly sliced, to garnish

1 Cut the pickled mustard leaves into bitesize pieces. Taste to check the seasoning. If they are too salty, soak them for a little longer.

2 Drain the cellophane noodles, discarding the soaking water, and cut them into pieces about 5cm/2in long.

3 Heat the oil in a small frying pan, add the garlic and stir-fry until golden. Transfer to a bowl and set aside.

4 Pour the chicken stock into a large pan, bring to the boil, then add the pork ribs and simmer gently over a low heat for about 10–15 minutes.

5 Add the pickled mustard leaves and cellophane noodles. Bring back to the boil. Season to taste with fish sauce, sugar and ground black pepper.

6 Pour the soup into individual serving bowls. Garnish with the fried garlic and the red chillies and serve hot.

Stock for Chinese Soups

This stock is an excellent basis for delicate Chinese soups.

INGREDIENTS

Makes 2.5 litres/4½ pints/11 cups

675g/1½lb chicken portions

675g/1½lb pork spareribs

3.75 litres/6 pints/16 cups water

3–4 pieces fresh root ginger, unpeeled and crushed

3–4 spring onions (scallions), each tied into a knot

45–60ml/3–4 tbsp Chinese rice wine

1 Trim off any excess fat from the chicken and spareribs and chop them into large pieces.

2 Place the chicken and sparerib pieces in a large stockpot with the water. Add the ginger and spring onion knots.

3 Bring to the boil and, using a sieve, skim off the froth. Reduce the heat and simmer, uncovered, for 2–3 hours.

4 Strain the stock, discarding the chicken, pork, ginger and spring onions. Add the rice wine and return to the boil. Simmer for 2–3 minutes. Store the stock in the refrigerator when it has cooled. It will keep for up to 4–5 days. Alternatively, it can be frozen in small containers and thawed when it is required.

Duck Consommé

The Vietnamese community in France has had a profound influence on French cooking, as this soup bears witness – it is light and rich at the same time, with intriguing flavours of South-east Asia.

INGREDIENTS

Serves 4

1 duck carcass (raw or cooked), plus 2 legs or any giblets, trimmed of as much fat as possible

1 large onion, unpeeled, with root end trimmed

2 carrots, cut into 5cm/2in pieces

1 parsnip, cut into 5cm/2in pieces

1 leek, cut into 5cm/2in pieces

2–4 garlic cloves, crushed

2.5cm/1in piece fresh root ginger, sliced

15ml/1 tbsp black peppercorns

4–6 fresh thyme sprigs or 5ml/1 tsp dried thyme

6–8 fresh coriander (cilantro) sprigs, leaves and stems separated

For the garnish

1 small carrot

1 small leek, halved lengthways

4–6 shiitake mushrooms, thinly sliced

soy sauce

2 spring onions (scallions), thinly sliced

watercress or finely shredded Chinese leaves (Chinese cabbage)

ground black pepper

1 Put the duck carcass and legs or giblets, onion, carrots, parsnip, leek and garlic in a large, heavy pan or flameproof casserole. Add the ginger, peppercorns, thyme and coriander stems, cover with cold water and bring to the boil over a medium-high heat, skimming off any foam that rises to the surface.

2 Reduce the heat and simmer gently for 1½–2 hours, then strain through a sieve lined with muslin (cheesecloth) into a bowl. Discard the bones and vegetables. Cool the stock and chill for several hours. Skim off any congealed fat and blot the surface with kitchen paper to remove any traces of fat.

3 To make the garnish, cut the carrot and leek into 5cm/2in pieces. Cut each piece lengthways into thin slices, then stack and slice into thin julienne strips. Place the carrot and leek strips in a large pan with the sliced mushrooms.

4 Pour over the stock and add a few dashes of soy sauce and some pepper. Bring to the boil over a medium-high heat, skimming any foam that rises to the surface. Adjust the seasoning if necessary. Stir in the spring onions and watercress or Chinese leaves. Ladle the consommé into warmed bowls and sprinkle with the coriander leaves before serving.

Stock for Japanese Soups

Dashi *is the stock that gives the characteristically Japanese flavour to many dishes. Known as* Ichiban-dashi, *it is used for delicately flavoured dishes, including soups. Of course instant stock is available in all Japanese supermarkets, either in granule form, in concentrate or even in a tea-bag style. Follow the instructions on the packet.*

INGREDIENTS

Makes about 800ml/1¹⁄₃ pints/3¹⁄₂ cups
10g/¹⁄₄oz dried kombu seaweed
10–15g/¹⁄₄–¹⁄₂oz bonito flakes

VARIATION
～
For vegetarian dashi, just omit the bonito flakes (dried tuna) and follow the same method.

1 Wipe the kombu seaweed with a damp cloth and cut two slits in it with scissors, so that it flavours the stock effectively.

2 Soak the kombu in 900ml/ 1¹⁄₂ pints/3³⁄₄ cups cold water for 30–60 minutes.

3 Heat the kombu in its soaking water over a moderate heat. Just before the water boils, remove the seaweed. Then add the bonito flakes and bring to the boil over a high heat, then remove the pan from the heat.

4 Leave the stock until all the bonito flakes have sunk to the base of the pan. Line a strainer with kitchen paper or muslin (cheesecloth) and place it over a large bowl, then gently strain.

Clear Soup with Meatballs

A Chinese-style soup, in which meatballs are combined with lightly cooked vegetables in a tasty stock.

INGREDIENTS

Serves 8

4–6 Chinese mushrooms, soaked in warm
    water for 30 minutes
30ml/2 tbsp groundnut (peanut) oil
1 large onion, finely chopped
2 garlic cloves, finely crushed
1cm/½in piece fresh root ginger, bruised
2 litres/3½ pints/9 cups Meat or Chicken
    stock, including the soaking liquid from
    the mushrooms
30ml/2 tbsp soy sauce
115g/4 oz curly kale, spinach or Chinese
    leaves (Chinese cabbage), shredded

For the meatballs

175g/6oz/¾ cup minced (ground) beef
1 small onion, finely chopped
1–2 garlic cloves, crushed
15ml/1 tbsp cornflour (cornstarch)
a little egg white, lightly beaten
salt and ground black pepper

1 First prepare the meatballs. Mix the beef with the onion, garlic, cornflour and seasoning in a food processor and then bind with sufficient egg white to make a firm mixture. With wet hands, roll into tiny, bitesize balls and set aside.

2 Drain the mushrooms. Reserve the soaking liquid. Trim off and discard the stalks. Slice the caps thinly and set aside.

3 Heat a wok or large pan and add the oil. Cook the onion, garlic and ginger to bring out the flavour, but do not allow to brown.

4 When the onion is soft, pour in the stock. Bring to the boil, then stir in the soy sauce and mushroom slices and simmer for 10 minutes. Add the meatballs and cook for 10 minutes.

5 Just before serving, remove the ginger. Stir in the shredded curly kale, spinach or Chinese leaves. Heat through for 1 minute only – no longer or the leaves will be overcooked. Ladle the soup into warm bowls and serve.

Garnishes

Sometimes, a soup needs something to lift it out of the ordinary, and garnishes are the answer. They are an important finishing touch; they not only look good, but also add an extra dimension to the flavour. A garnish can be as simple as a sprinkling of chopped parsley, a swirl of cream or some freshly grated cheese. Alternatively, it can be something that requires a little more attention, such as home-made croûtons or sippets. All the garnishes featured here are suitable for vegetarian soups.

DUMPLINGS

These dumplings are easy to make and add an attractive and tasty finishing touch to country soups.

INGREDIENTS

75g/3oz/½ cup semolina or flour
1 egg, beaten
45ml/3 tbsp milk or water
generous pinch of salt
15ml/1 tbsp chopped fresh parsley

1 Combine all the ingredients into a soft, elastic dough. Leave to stand, covered with clear film (plastic wrap), for 10 minutes.

2 Drop small rounded dessert-spoonfuls of this mixture into the soup and cook for 10 minutes, until firm.

CRISPY CROÛTONS

Croûtons add a lovely crunchy texture to creamy soups and are a good way of using up stale bread. Use thinly sliced ciabatta or French bread for delicious results.

INGREDIENTS

bread
good quality, flavourless oil, such as sunflower or groundnut (peanut) or, for a fuller flavour, extra virgin olive oil or a flavoured oil, such as one with garlic and herbs or chilli

1 Preheat the oven to 200°C/400°F/Gas 6. Cut the bread into small cubes and place on a baking sheet.

2 Brush with your chosen oil, then bake for 15 minutes, until golden and crisp. Leave to cool slightly: they crisp up further as they cool down.

3 Store them in an airtight container for up to a week. Reheat in a warm oven, if you like, before serving.

RIVELS

Rivels are pea-size pieces of dough which swell when cooked in a soup.

INGREDIENTS

1 egg
75–115g/3–4oz/¾–1 cup flour
2.5ml/½ tsp salt
freshly ground black pepper

1 Beat the egg in a bowl. Add the flour, salt and pepper to taste and mix with a wooden spoon. Finish mixing with your fingers, rubbing to blend the egg and flour together to form pea-size pieces.

2 Bring the soup back to the boil. Sprinkle in the pieces of dough, stirring gently.

3 Reduce the heat and simmer for about 6 minutes, until the rivels are slightly swollen and cooked through. Serve the garnished soup immediately.

Chinese Chicken and Asparagus Soup

This is a very delicate and delicious soup. When fresh asparagus is not in season, canned white asparagus is an acceptable substitute.

INGREDIENTS

Serves 4

140g/5oz skinless, boneless chicken
   breast portion
5ml/1 tsp egg white
5ml/1 tsp cornflour (cornstarch) mixed to
   a paste with 15ml/1 tbsp water
115g/4oz asparagus
700ml/1¼ pints/3 cups Chicken Stock
salt and ground black pepper
fresh coriander (cilantro) , to garnish

1 Cut the chicken into very thin slices each about 4 × 2.5cm/ 1½ × 1in. Mix with a pinch of salt, then add the egg white, and finally the cornflour paste.

2 Cut off and discard the tough stems of the asparagus, and cut the tender spears diagonally into short, even lengths.

3 In a wok or pan, bring the stock to a rolling boil, add the asparagus, bring back to the boil and cook for 2 minutes. (You do not need to do this if you are using canned asparagus.)

4 Add the chicken, stir to separate and bring back to the boil once more. Taste and adjust the seasoning if necessary. Serve immediately, garnished with fresh coriander leaves.

SWIRLED CREAM

An attractive swirl of cream is the classic finish for many soups, such as a smooth tomato soup and chilled asparagus soup. The garnish gives a delightfully professional finish to your soup, although the technique is simplicity itself.

INGREDIENTS

single (light) cream

1 Transfer the cream into a jug (pitcher). Pour a swirl on to the surface of each bowl of soup.

2 Draw the tip of a fine skewer quickly backwards and forwards through the cream to create a delicate pattern. Serve the soup immediately.

SIPPETS

Another good way of using up slightly stale bread, sippets are larger than croûtons and have a more intense flavour because of the addition of fresh herbs. Experiment with the herbs according to the flavour of the soup.

INGREDIENTS

3 slices day-old bread
50g/2 oz/4 tbsp butter
45ml/3 tbsp finely chopped fresh parsley, or coriander (cilantro) or basil

1 Cut the bread into fingers about 2.5cm/1in long.

2 Melt the butter in a large frying pan, toss in the small fingers of bread and cook gently until golden brown.

3 Add the fresh herbs and stir well to combine. Cook for a further minute, stirring constantly. Sprinkle the sippets on top of the soup and serve.

LEEK HAYSTACKS

Stacks of golden leek look good served on a creamy soup and the crunchy texture contrasts well with the smoothness of the soup.

INGREDIENTS

1 large leek
30ml/2 tbsp plain (all-purpose) flour
oil, for deep-frying

1 Slice the leek in half lengthways and then cut into quarters. Cut into 5cm/2in lengths and then into very fine strips. Place in a bowl, sprinkle the flour over and toss to coat.

2 Heat the oil to 160ºC/325ºF. Drop small spoonfuls of the floured leeks into the oil and cook for 30–45 seconds, until golden. Drain on kitchen paper. Repeat with the remaining leeks.

3 Serve the soup with a small stack of leeks piled on top of each bowl.

Wonton Soup

In China, wonton soup is served as a snack, or dim sum, but is a popular soup course in the West.

INGREDIENTS

Serves 4

175g/6oz pork, coarsely chopped

50g/2oz peeled prawns (shrimp), finely chopped

5ml/1 tsp light brown sugar

15ml/1 tbsp Chinese rice wine

15ml/1 tbsp light soy sauce

5ml/1 tsp finely chopped spring onions (scallions), plus extra to garnish

5ml/1 tsp finely chopped fresh root ginger

24 ready-made wonton skins

about 750ml/1¼ pints/3 cups Stock for Chinese Soups

15ml/1 tbsp light soy sauce

1 In a bowl, mix the pork and prawns with the sugar, rice wine, soy sauce, spring onions and ginger. Set aside for 25–30 minutes for the flavours to blend.

2 Place about 5ml/1 tsp of the pork mixture in the centre of each wonton skin.

3 Wet the edges of each filled wonton skin with a little water and press them together with your fingers to seal. Fold each wonton parcel over.

4 To cook, bring the stock to a rolling boil in a wok, add the wontons and cook for 4–5 minutes. Season with the soy sauce and add the extra spring onions.

5 Transfer to individual soup bowls and serve.

CHILLED
SOUPS

Indian Beef and Berry Soup

The fresh berries give this soup a pleasant kick.

INGREDIENTS

Serves 4

30ml/2 tbsp vegetable oil

450g/1lb tender beef steak

2 onions, thinly sliced

25g/1oz/2 tbsp butter

1 litre/1¾ pints/4 cups Meat Stock

2.5ml/½ tsp salt

115g/4oz/1 cup fresh huckleberries,
  blueberries or blackberries,
  lightly mashed

15ml/1 tbsp clear honey

1 Heat the oil in a heavy pan until almost smoking. Add the steak and cook on both sides over a medium-high heat until well browned. Remove the steak from the pan and set aside.

2 Reduce the heat to low and add the sliced onions and butter to the pan. Stir thoroughly, scraping up the meat juices. Cook over a low heat for 8–10 minutes, until the onions are softened.

3 Add the meat stock and salt and bring to the boil, stirring constantly. Mix in the mashed berries and the honey. Simmer for 20 minutes.

4 Cut the steak into thin slivers. Taste the soup and add more salt or honey if necessary. Add the steak to the pan. Cook gently for 30 seconds, stirring, then serve.

Almond Soup

Unless you are prepared to spend time pounding all the ingredients for this soup by hand, a food processor is essential. Then you'll find that this Spanish soup is simple to make and refreshing to eat on a hot summer's day.

INGREDIENTS

Serves 6

115g/4 oz fresh white bread
750ml/1¼ pints/3 cups water
115g/4oz/1 cup blanched almonds
2 garlic cloves, sliced
75ml/5 tbsp olive oil
25ml/1½ tbsp sherry vinegar
salt and ground black pepper

For the garnish
toasted flaked (sliced) almonds
seedless green and black grapes, halved
  and skinned

1 Break the bread into a bowl and pour 150ml/¼ pint/ ⅔ cup of the water on top. Leave for 5 minutes.

2 Put the almonds and garlic in a blender or food processor and process until finely ground. Blend in the soaked bread.

3 Gradually add the oil until the mixture forms a smooth paste. Add the sherry vinegar, then the remaining cold water and process until smooth.

4 Transfer to a bowl and season with salt and pepper, adding a little more water if the soup is too thick. Chill for at least 2–3 hours. Serve sprinkled with the toasted almonds and grapes.

Jalapeño-style Soup

Chicken, chilli and avocado combine to make this simple but unusual soup.

INGREDIENTS

Serves 6

1.5 litres/2½ pints/6¼ cups Chicken Stock

2 cooked chicken breast fillets, skinned and cut into large strips

1 drained canned chipotle or jalapeño chilli, rinsed

1 avocado

COOK'S TIP

When using canned chillies, it is important to rinse them thoroughly before adding them to a dish in order to remove the flavour of any pickling liquid.

1 Heat the stock in a large pan and add the chicken and chilli. Simmer over a very gentle heat for 5 minutes to heat the chicken through and release the flavour from the chilli.

2 Cut the avocado in half, remove the stone (pit) and peel off the skin. Slice the avocado flesh neatly lengthways.

3 Using a slotted spoon, remove the chilli from the pan and discard it. Pour the soup into heated serving bowls, distributing the chicken evenly among them.

4 Add a few avocado slices to each bowl and serve.

Tomato and Sweet Pepper Soup

This recipe was inspired by the Spanish gazpacho, the difference being that this soup is cooked first, and then chilled.

INGREDIENTS

Serves 4

2 red (bell) peppers, halved and seeded

45ml/3 tbsp olive oil

1 onion, finely chopped

2 garlic cloves, crushed

675g/1½lb ripe well-flavoured tomatoes

150ml/¼ pint/⅔ cup red wine

600ml/1 pint/2½ cups Chicken Stock

salt and ground black pepper

chopped fresh chives, to garnish

For the croûtons

2 slices white bread, crusts removed

60ml/4 tbsp olive oil

1 Cut each red pepper half into quarters. Place skin side up on a grill (broiler) rack and cook until the skins are charred. Transfer to a bowl and cover with a plate or pop into a plastic bag and seal.

2 Heat the oil in a large pan. Add the onion and garlic and cook gently until soft. Meanwhile, remove the skin from the peppers and coarsely chop the flesh. Cut the tomatoes into chunks.

3 Add the peppers and tomatoes to the pan, then cover and cook gently for 10 minutes. Add the wine and cook for a further 5 minutes, then add the stock and salt and pepper and continue to simmer for 20 minutes.

4 To make the croûtons, cut the bread into cubes. Heat the oil in a small frying pan, add the bread and cook until golden. Drain on kitchen paper and store in an airtight box.

5 Process the soup in a blender or food processor until smooth. Pour into a clean glass or ceramic bowl and leave to cool thoroughly before chilling in the refrigerator for at least 3 hours. When the soup is cold, season to taste with salt and pepper.

6 Serve the soup in bowls, topped with the croûtons and garnished with chopped chives.

Spicy Chicken and Mushroom Soup

This creamy chicken soup makes a wonderful start to a meal.

INGREDIENTS

Serves 4

75g/3oz/6 tbsp unsalted (sweet) butter

2.5ml/½ tsp crushed garlic

5ml/1 tsp garam masala

5ml/1 tsp crushed black peppercorns

5ml/1 tsp salt

1.5ml/¼ tsp freshly grated nutmeg

225g/8oz skinless, boneless chicken
    breast portions

1 medium leek, sliced

75g/3 oz/generous 1 cup
    mushrooms, sliced

50g/2 oz/⅓ cup corn kernels

300ml/½ pint/1¼ cups water

250ml/8fl oz/1 cup single (light) cream

30ml/2 tbsp chopped fresh
    coriander (cilantro)

5ml/1 tsp crushed dried red chillies, to
    garnish (optional)

1 Melt the butter in a pan. Lower the heat slightly and add the garlic and garam masala. Lower the heat further and add the peppercorns, salt and nutmeg.

2 Cut the chicken pieces into very fine strips and add to the pan with the leek, mushrooms and corn. Cook for 5–7 minutes, until the chicken is cooked through, stirring constantly.

3 Remove from the heat and leave to cool slightly. Transfer three-quarters of the mixture to a food processor or blender. Add the water and process for about 1 minute.

4 Pour the resulting purée back into the pan with the rest of the mixture and bring to the boil over a medium heat. Lower the heat and stir in the cream.

5 Add the fresh coriander. Taste and adjust the seasoning. Serve hot, garnished with crushed red chillies, if you like.

Gazpacho with Avocado Salsa

Tomatoes, cucumber and peppers form the basis of this classic, chilled soup. Add a spoonful of chunky, fresh avocado salsa and a small sprinkling of croûtons for a delicious summer appetizer. This is quite a substantial soup, so follow with a light main course, such as grilled fish or chicken.

INGREDIENTS

Serves 4–6

2 slices day-old bread
600ml/1 pint/2½ cups chilled water
1kg/2¼ lb tomatoes
1 cucumber
1 red (bell) pepper, seeded and chopped
1 green chilli, seeded and chopped
2 garlic cloves, chopped
30ml/2 tbsp extra virgin olive oil
juice of 1 lime and 1 lemon
few drops of Tabasco sauce
salt and ground black pepper
handful of fresh basil, to garnish
8–12 ice cubes, to serve

For the croûtons
2–3 slices day-old bread, crusts removed
1 garlic clove, halved
15–30ml/1–2 tbsp olive oil

For the avocado salsa
1 ripe avocado
5ml/1 tsp lemon juice
2.5cm/1in piece cucumber, diced
½ red chilli, seeded and finely chopped

1 Make the soup first. In a shallow bowl, soak the day-old bread in 150ml/¼ pint/⅔ cup water for 5 minutes.

COOK'S TIP

For a superior flavour choose Haas avocados with the rough-textured, almost black skins.

---

2 Meanwhile, place the tomatoes in a heatproof bowl; cover with boiling water. Leave for 30 seconds, then peel, seed and chop the flesh.

3 Thinly peel the cucumber, cut in half lengthways and scoop out the seeds with a teaspoon. Discard the seeds and chop the flesh.

4 Place the bread, tomatoes, cucumber, red pepper, chilli, garlic, oil, citrus juices, Tabasco and 450ml/¾ pint/scant 2 cups chilled water in a food processor or blender. Blend until mixed but still chunky. Season and chill well.

5 To make the croûtons, rub the slices of bread with the cut surface of the garlic clove. Cut the bread into cubes and place in a plastic bag with the olive oil. Seal the bag and shake until the bread cubes are coated with the oil. Heat a large non-stick frying pan and cook the croûtons over a medium heat until crisp and golden.

6 Just before serving make the avocado salsa. Halve the avocado, remove the stone (pit), then peel and dice the flesh. Toss the avocado in the lemon juice to prevent it from browning, then mix with the cucumber and chilli.

7 Ladle the soup into bowls, add the ice cubes and top with a spoonful of avocado salsa. Garnish with the basil and hand around the croûtons separately.

Lamb and Lentil Soup

Lamb and red lentils go together so well, they seem to have been made for one another.

INGREDIENTS

Serves 4

about 1.5 litres/2½ pints/6¼ cups water
900g/2lb neck (US shoulder or breast) of
    lamb, cut into chops
½ onion, chopped
1 garlic clove, crushed
1 bay leaf
1 clove
2 fresh thyme sprigs
225g/8oz potatoes, cut into 2.5cm/
    1in pieces
175g/6oz/¾ cup red lentils
salt and ground black pepper
chopped fresh parsley

1 Put about 1.2 litres/2 pints/ 5 cups of the water and the meat in a large pan with the onion, garlic, bay leaf, clove and sprigs of thyme. Bring to the boil, lower the heat and simmer for about 1 hour, until the lamb is tender.

VARIATION

For a richer, fuller flavour, substitute Meat Stock, made with lamb bones, or Chicken Stock for all of some of the water.

2 Add the pieces of potato and the lentils to the pan and season the soup with a little salt and plenty of black pepper. Add the remaining water to come just above surface of the meat and vegetables; you may need to add more if the soup becomes too thick during cooking.

3 Cover and simmer for about 25 minutes, or until the lentils are cooked and well blended into the soup. Taste the soup and adjust the seasoning as necessary. Stir in the parsley and serve.

Cucumber and Yogurt Soup with Walnuts

This is a particularly refreshing cold soup, using a classic combination of cucumber and yogurt.

INGREDIENTS

Serves 5–6

1 cucumber

4 garlic cloves

2.5ml/½ tsp salt

75g/3oz/¾ cup walnut pieces

40g/1½oz day-old bread, torn into pieces

30ml/2 tbsp walnut or sunflower oil

400ml/14fl oz/1⅔ cups natural (plain) yogurt

120ml/4fl oz/½ cup cold water

5–10ml/1–2 tsp lemon juice

For the garnish

40g/1½oz/scant ½ cup walnuts, coarsely chopped

25ml/1½ tbsp olive oil

fresh dill sprigs

1 Cut the cucumber in half and peel one half of it. Dice the cucumber flesh and set aside.

2 Using a large mortar and pestle, crush together the garlic and salt well, then add the walnuts and bread.

3 When the mixture is smooth, gradually add the walnut or sunflower oil and combine well.

COOK'S TIP

If you prefer your soup smooth, process it in a food processor or blender before serving.

4 Transfer the mixture to a large bowl and beat in the yogurt and diced cucumber. Add the cold water and then stir in lemon juice to taste.

5 Pour the soup into chilled soup bowls to serve. Garnish with the chopped walnuts and drizzle with the olive oil. Finally, arrange the sprigs of dill on top and serve immediately.

Chicken, Tomato and Christophine Soup

Chicken breast portions and smoked haddock take on the flavours of herbs and spices to produce this tasty soup.

INGREDIENTS

Serves 4

225g/8oz skinless, boneless chicken breast portions, diced

1 garlic clove, crushed

pinch of freshly grated nutmeg

25g/1oz/2 tbsp butter or margarine

½ onion, finely chopped

15ml/1 tbsp tomato purée (paste)

400g/14 oz can tomatoes, puréed

1.2 litres/2 pints/5 cups Chicken Stock

1 fresh chilli, seeded and chopped

1 christophine, peeled and diced (about 350g/12oz)

5ml/1 tsp dried oregano

2.5ml/½ tsp dried thyme

50g/2oz smoked haddock fillet, skinned and diced

salt and ground black pepper

chopped fresh chives, to garnish

1 Dice the chicken, place in a bowl and season with salt, pepper, garlic and nutmeg. Mix well to flavour and then set aside for about 30 minutes.

2 Melt the butter or margarine in a large pan, add the chicken and sauté over a moderate heat for 5–6 minutes. Stir in the onion and cook gently, stirring frequently, for a further 5 minutes, or until the onion is slightly softened.

3 Add the tomato purée, puréed tomatoes, chicken stock, chilli, christophine, oregano and thyme. Bring to the boil, lower the heat, cover and simmer gently for about 35 minutes, or until the chicken and christophine are tender.

4 Add the smoked haddock and simmer for 5 minutes more, or until the fish is cooked through. Adjust the seasoning and pour into warmed soup bowls. Garnish with a sprinkling of chopped fresh chives and serve piping hot.

Green Pea and Mint Soup

Perfect partners, peas and mint really capture the flavours of summer.

INGREDIENTS

Serves 4

50g/2oz/4 tbsp butter

4 spring onions (scallions), chopped

450g/1lb fresh or frozen peas

600ml/1 pint/2½ cups Vegetable Stock

2 large fresh mint sprigs

600ml/1 pint/2½ cups milk

pinch of sugar (optional)

salt and ground black pepper

small fresh mint sprigs, to garnish

single (light) cream, to serve

1 Heat the butter in a large pan, add the chopped spring onions and cook gently on a low heat until they are softened, but not browned.

2 Stir the peas into the pan, add the stock and mint and bring to the boil. Cover and simmer gently for about 30 minutes if you are using fresh peas (15 minutes if you are using frozen peas), until they are tender. Remove about 45ml/3 tbsp of the peas, and set aside to use for a garnish.

3 Pour the soup into a food processor or blender, add the milk and process until smooth. Season to taste, adding a pinch of sugar, if you like. Leave to cool, then chill lightly in the refrigerator.

4 Pour the soup into bowls. Swirl a little cream into each, then garnish with the mint and the reserved peas.

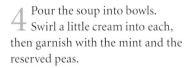

Onion and Pancetta Soup

This warming winter soup comes from Umbria in Italy, where it is sometimes thickened with beaten eggs and plenty of grated Parmesan cheese. It is then served on top of hot toasted croûtes – rather like savoury scrambled eggs.

INGREDIENTS

Serves 4

115g/4oz pancetta rashers (strips), rinds
  removed, coarsely chopped
30ml/2 tbsp olive oil
15g/¹/₂oz/1 tbsp butter
675g/1¹/₂lb onions, thinly sliced
10ml/2 tsp granulated sugar
about 1.2 litres/2 pints/5 cups
  Chicken Stock
350g/12oz ripe Italian plum tomatoes,
  peeled and coarsely chopped
few fresh basil leaves, shredded
salt and ground black pepper
grated Parmesan cheese, to serve

1 Put the chopped pancetta in a large pan and heat gently, stirring constantly, until the fat runs. Increase the heat to medium, add the olive oil, butter, sliced onions and granulated sugar and stir well to mix.

2 Half-cover the pan and cook the onions gently for about 20 minutes, until golden. Stir frequently and lower the heat if necessary.

3 Add the stock and tomatoes, season to taste with salt and pepper and bring to the boil, stirring constantly. Lower the heat, half-cover the pan and simmer, stirring occasionally, for about 30 minutes.

4 Check the consistency of the soup and add a little more stock or water if it is too thick.

5 Just before serving, stir in most of the basil and taste adjust the seasoning if necessary. Serve immediately, garnished with the remaining shredded basil. Hand around the freshly grated Parmesan separately.

COOK'S TIP

Look for Vidalia onions to make this soup. They are available at large supermarkets, and have a sweet flavour and attractive, yellowish flesh.

Watercress and Orange Soup

This is a healthy and refreshing soup, which is just as good served either hot or chilled.

INGREDIENTS

Serves 4

1 large onion, chopped

15ml/1 tbsp olive oil

2 bunches or bags of watercress

grated rind and juice of 1 large orange

600ml/1 pint/2½ cups Vegetable Stock

150ml/¼ pint/⅔ cup single (light) cream

10ml/2 tsp cornflour (cornstarch)

salt and ground black pepper

a little thick cream or natural (plain)
   yogurt, to garnish

4 orange wedges, to serve

1 Soften the onion in the oil in a large pan. Add the watercress, unchopped, to the onion. Cover and cook for about 5 minutes, until the watercress is wilted.

2 Add the orange rind and juice and the stock to the watercress mixture. Bring to the boil, then lower the heat, cover and simmer for 10–15 minutes.

3 Process the soup thoroughly in a blender or food processor and sieve if you want to increase the smoothness of the finished soup. Blend the cream with the cornflour until no lumps remain, then add to the soup. Season to taste with salt and pepper.

4 Bring the soup gently back to the boil, stirring constantly until just slightly thickened. Check the seasoning.

5 Leave the soup to cool, then chill in the refrigerator. Serve the soup with a swirl of cream or yogurt, and a wedge of orange to squeeze in at the last moment.

6 If serving the soup hot, garnish with a swirl of cream or yogurt and orange wedges, as above, and serve immediately.

Galician Broth

This delicious Spanish soup is very similar to the warming, chunky meat and potato broths of cooler climates. For extra colour, a few onion skins can be added when cooking the gammon, but remember to remove them before serving.

INGREDIENTS

Serves 4

450g/1lb piece gammon (cured ham)
2 bay leaves
2 onions, sliced
1.5 litres/2½ pints/6¼ cups water
10ml/2 tsp paprika
675g/1½ lb potatoes, cut into large chunks
225g/8oz spring greens (collards)
400g/14oz can haricot (navy) or cannellini beans, drained and rinsed
salt and ground black pepper

1 Soak the gammon overnight in cold water. Drain and put in a large pan with the bay leaves and onions. Pour the water on top.

2 Bring to the boil, then reduce the heat and simmer gently for about 1½ hours, until the meat is tender. Keep an eye on the pan to make sure it doesn't boil over.

COOK'S TIP
~

Bacon knuckles can be used instead of the gammon (cured ham). The bones will give the juices a delicious flavour.

3 Drain the meat, reserving the cooking liquid, and leave to cool slightly. Discard the skin and any excess fat from the meat and cut into small chunks. Return to the pan with the paprika and potatoes. Cover and simmer gently for 20 minutes.

4 Cut away the cores from the greens. Roll up the leaves and cut into thin shreds. Add to the pan with the beans and simmer for about 10 minutes. Season with salt and ground black pepper to taste. Ladle into warm soup bowls and serve piping hot.

Hungarian Sour Cherry Soup

Particularly popular in summer, this fruit soup is typical of Hungarian cooking. The recipe makes good use of plump, sour cherries. Fruit soups are thickened with flour, and a touch of salt is added to help bring out the flavour of the cold soup.

INGREDIENTS

Serves 4

15ml/1 tbsp plain (all-purpose) flour

120ml/4fl oz/½ cup sour cream

a generous pinch of salt

5ml/1 tsp caster (superfine) sugar

225g/8oz/1½ cups fresh sour or morello
    cherries, pitted

900ml/1½ pints/3¾ cups water

50g/2oz/¼ cup granulated sugar

1 In a bowl, blend the flour with the sour cream until completely smooth, then add the salt and caster sugar.

2 Put the cherries in a pan with the water and granulated sugar. Gently poach for about 10 minutes.

3 Remove from the heat and set aside 30ml/2 tbsp of the cooking liquid as a garnish. Stir another 30ml/2 tbsp of the cherry liquid into the flour and sour cream mixture, then pour this on to the cherries.

4 Return to the heat. Bring to the boil, then simmer gently for 5–6 minutes.

5 Remove from the heat, cover with clear film (plastic wrap) and leave to cool. Add extra salt if necessary. Serve with the reserved cooking liquid swirled in.

Mulligatawny Soup

Mulligatawny *(which literally means "pepper water") was introduced into England in the late eighteenth century by members of the colonial services returning home from India.*

INGREDIENTS

Serves 4

50 g/2 oz/4 tbsp butter or 60 ml/4 tbsp oil

2 large chicken joints (about 350 g/12 oz each)

1 onion, chopped

1 carrot, chopped

1 small turnip, chopped

about 15 ml/1 tbsp curry powder, to taste

4 cloves

6 black peppercorns, lightly crushed

50 g/2 oz/¼ cup lentils

900 ml/1½ pints/3¾ cups chicken stock

40 g/1½ oz/¼ cup sultanas (golden raisins)

salt and freshly ground black pepper

1 Melt the butter or heat the oil in a large pan, then brown the chicken over a brisk heat. Transfer the chicken to a plate and set aside.

2 Add the onion, carrot and turnip to the pan and cook, stirring occasionally, until lightly coloured. Stir in the curry powder, cloves and crushed peppercorns and cook for 1–2 minutes, then add the lentils.

3 Pour the stock into the pan, bring to the boil, then add the sultanas, the chicken and any juices from the plate. Cover and simmer gently for about 1¼ hours.

COOK'S TIP

Choose red split lentils for the best colour, although either green or brown lentils could also be used.

4 Remove the chicken from the pan and discard the skin and bones. Chop the flesh, return to the soup and reheat. Check the seasoning before serving the soup piping hot.

Melon and Basil Soup

This is a deliciously refreshing, fruit soup, just right for a hot day.

INGREDIENTS

Serves 4–6

2 Charentais or rock melons

75g/3oz/scant ½ cup caster
   (superfine) sugar

175ml/6fl oz/¾ cup water

finely grated rind and juice of 1 lime

45ml/3 tbsp shredded fresh basil, plus
   whole leaves, to garnish

2 Place the sugar, water and lime rind in a small pan over a low heat. Stir until dissolved, bring to the boil and simmer gently for 2–3 minutes. Remove from the heat and leave to cool slightly. Pour half the mixture into the blender or food processor with the melon flesh. Blend until smooth, adding the remaining syrup and lime juice to taste.

3 Pour the mixture into a bowl, stir in the shredded basil and chill in the refrigerator. Serve garnished with whole basil leaves and the reserved melon balls.

1 Cut the melons in half across the middle. Scrape out the seeds and discard. Using a melon baller, scoop out 20–24 balls and set aside for the garnish. Scoop out the remaining flesh and place in a blender or food processor.

COOK'S TIP

Add the syrup in two stages, as the amount of sugar needed will depend on the sweetness of the melon.

Chicken Minestrone

This is a special minestrone made with fresh chicken. Serve with crusty Italian bread.

INGREDIENTS

Serves 4–6

15ml/1 tbsp olive oil

2 chicken thighs

3 rindless streaky (fatty) bacon rashers (strips) , chopped

1 onion, finely chopped

few fresh basil leaves, shredded

few fresh rosemary leaves, finely chopped

15ml/1 tbsp chopped fresh flat leaf parsley

2 potatoes, cut into 1cm/$\frac{1}{2}$in cubes

1 large carrot, cut into 1cm/$\frac{1}{2}$in cubes

2 small courgettes (zucchini), cut into 1cm/$\frac{1}{2}$in cubes

1–2 celery sticks, cut into 1cm/$\frac{1}{2}$in cubes

1 litre/1$\frac{3}{4}$ pints/4 cups Chicken Stock

200g/7oz/1$\frac{3}{4}$ cups frozen peas

90g/3$\frac{1}{2}$oz/scant 1 cup stellette or other small soup pasta

salt and ground black pepper

Parmesan cheese shavings, to serve

1 Heat the oil in a large frying pan, add the chicken thighs and cook over a medium heat for about 5 minutes on each side. Remove with a slotted spoon and set aside.

2 Add the bacon, onion and herbs to the pan and cook gently, stirring constantly, for about 5 minutes. Add the potatoes, carrot, courgettes and celery and cook for 5–7 minutes more.

3 Return the chicken thighs to the pan, add the stock and bring to the boil. Cover and cook over a low heat for 35–40 minutes, stirring the soup occasionally.

4 Remove the chicken thighs with a slotted spoon and place them on a board. Stir the peas and pasta into the soup and bring back to the boil. Simmer, stirring frequently, for 7–8 minutes or according to the instructions on the packet, until the pasta is just *al dente*.

5 Meanwhile, remove and discard the chicken skin, then remove the meat from the chicken bones and cut it into small (1cm/$\frac{1}{2}$in) pieces.

6 Return the meat to the soup, stir well and heat through. Taste and adjust the seasoning as necessary.

7 Ladle the soup into warmed soup plates or bowls, top with Parmesan shavings and serve immediately, while piping hot.

Asparagus Soup

This delicate, pale green soup, garnished with a swirl of cream or yogurt, is as pretty as it is delicious.

INGREDIENTS

Serves 6

900g/2lb fresh asparagus

60ml/4 tbsp butter or olive oil

175g/6oz/1½ cups sliced leeks or spring onions (scallions)

45ml/3 tbsp plain (all-purpose) flour

1.5 litres/2½ pints/6¼ cups Chicken Stock or water

120ml/4fl oz/½ cup single (light) cream or natural (plain) yogurt

15ml/1 tbsp chopped fresh tarragon or chervil

salt and ground black pepper

3 Heat the butter or oil in a heavy pan. Add the sliced leeks or spring onions and cook over a low heat, stirring occasionally, for 5–8 minutes, until softened, but not browned. Stir in the chopped asparagus stalks, cover and cook for a further 6–8 minutes, until the stalks are tender.

4 Add the flour and stir well to blend. Cook for 3–4 minutes, uncovered, stirring occasionally.

5 Add the stock or water. Bring to the boil, stirring frequently, then reduce the heat and simmer for 30 minutes. Season to taste with salt and pepper.

6 Process the soup in a food processor or food mill. If necessary, strain it to remove any coarse fibres. Stir in the asparagus tips, most of the cream or yogurt, and the herbs. Cool, then chill well. Stir before serving and check the seasoning. Garnish each bowl with a swirl of cream or yogurt.

1 Cut the top 6cm/2½in off the asparagus spears and blanch in boiling water for 5–6 minutes, until just tender. Drain thoroughly. Cut each tip into two or three pieces and set aside.

2 Trim the ends of the stalks, removing any brown or woody parts. Chop the stalks into 1cm/½in pieces.

Bulgarian Sour Lamb Soup

This traditional sour soup uses lamb, although pork and poultry are popular alternatives.

INGREDIENTS

Serves 4–5

30ml/2 tbsp oil
450g/1lb lean lamb, trimmed and cubed
1 onion, diced
30ml/2 tbsp plain (all-purpose) flour
15ml/l tbsp paprika
1 litre/1¾ pints/4 cups hot Meat Stock
3 fresh parsley sprigs
4 spring onions (scallions)
4 fresh dill sprigs
39ml/2 tbsp long grain rice
2 eggs, beaten
30–45ml/2–3 tbsp or more vinegar or
    lemon juice
salt and ground black pepper

For the garnish
25g/1oz/2 tbsp butter, melted
5ml/1 tsp paprika
a little fresh parsley or lovage and dill

1 In a large pan heat the oil and cook the meat over a medium heat, stirring frequently, for about 8 minutes, until browned all over. Add the diced onion and cook, stirring frequently, for 5 minutes until it has softened. Sprinkle in the flour and paprika. Stir well, then gradually add the stock and cook for 10 minutes.

2 Tie the parsley, spring onions and dill together with kitchen string to make a bouquet garni, then add to the pan with the rice and season to taste with salt and pepper. Bring to the boil, then reduce the heat and simmer for about 30–40 minutes, or until the lamb is tender.

3 Remove the pan from the heat and stir in the eggs. Add the vinegar or lemon juice. Discard the bouquet garni and season to taste.

4 For the garnish, melt the butter in a pan and stir in the paprika. Ladle the soup into warm serving bowls. Garnish with parsley or dill and lovage and a little red paprika butter and serve immediately.

Prawn and Cucumber Soup

If you've never served a chilled soup before, this is the one to try first. Delicious and light, it's the perfect way to celebrate summer.

INGREDIENTS

Serves 4

25g/1oz/2 tbsp butter
2 shallots, finely chopped
2 garlic cloves, crushed
1 cucumber, peeled, seeded and diced
300ml/½ pint/1¼ cups milk
225g/8oz cooked peeled prawns (shrimp)
15ml/1 tbsp each finely chopped fresh
   mint, dill, chives and chervil
300ml/½ pint/1¼ cups whipping cream
salt and ground white pepper

For the garnish
30ml/2 tbsp crème fraîche or sour
   cream (optional)
4 large, cooked prawns (shrimp), peeled
   with tails intact
fresh chives and dill

1 Melt the butter in a pan and cook the shallots and garlic over a low heat until soft but not coloured. Add the cucumber and cook the vegetables gently, stirring frequently, until tender.

2 Stir in the milk, bring almost to the boil, then lower the heat and simmer for 5 minutes. Tip the soup into a blender or food processor and process until very smooth. Season to taste with salt and ground white pepper.

3 Pour the soup into a bowl and set aside to cool. When cool, stir in the prawns, chopped herbs and the whipping cream. Cover, transfer to the refrigerator and chill for at least 2 hours.

4 To serve, ladle the soup into four chilled individual bowls and top each portion with a spoonful of crème fraîche or sour cream, if using. Place a large prawn over the edge of each soup bowl. Garnish with the chives and dill.

COOK'S TIP

For a change try fresh or canned crab meat, or cooked, flaked salmon fillet.

Chunky Chicken Soup

This thick chicken and vegetable soup is served with garlic-flavoured fried croûtons.

INGREDIENTS

Serves 4

4 skinless, boneless chicken thighs

15g/¹⁄₂oz/1 tbsp butter

2 small leeks, thinly sliced

30ml/2 tbsp long grain rice

900ml/ 1¹⁄₂ pints/3³⁄₄ cups Chicken Stock

15ml/1 tbsp chopped mixed fresh parsley
  and mint

salt and ground black pepper

For the garlic croûtons

30ml/2 tbsp olive oil

1 garlic clove, crushed

4 slices bread, cut into cubes

1 Cut the chicken into 1cm/ ¹⁄₂in cubes. Melt the butter in a pan, add the leeks and cook until tender. Add the rice and chicken and cook for 2 minutes.

2 Add the stock, then cover the pan and simmer gently for 15–20 minutes, until tender.

3 To make the garlic croûtons, heat the oil in a large frying pan. Add the crushed garlic clove and bread cubes and cook until the bread is golden brown, stirring constantly to prevent burning. Drain on kitchen paper and sprinkle with a pinch of salt.

4 Add the parsley and mint to the soup and adjust the seasoning to taste. Serve with the garlic croûtons.

Gazpacho

This is a traditional, chilled Spanish soup, perfect for a summer lunch. Make sure that all the ingredients are in peak condition for the best-flavoured soup.

INGREDIENTS

Serves 6

1 green (bell) pepper, seeded and chopped

1 red (bell) pepper, seeded and chopped

½ cucumber, roughly chopped

1 onion, roughly chopped

1 fresh red chilli, seeded and roughly chopped

450g/1lb ripe plum tomatoes, roughly chopped

900ml/1½ pints/3¾ cups passata or tomato juice

30ml/2 tbsp red wine vinegar

30ml/2 tbsp olive oil

15ml/1 tbsp caster (superfine) sugar

salt and freshly ground black pepper

crushed ice, to garnish (optional)

1 Reserve a small piece of green and red pepper, cucumber and onion. Finely chop these and set aside as a garnish.

2 Process all the remaining ingredients (except the ice) in a blender or food processor until smooth. You may need to do this in batches.

3 Pass the soup through a sieve into a clean glass bowl, pushing it through with a spoon to extract the maximum amount of flavour.

4 Adjust the seasoning and chill. Serve sprinkled with the reserved chopped green and red pepper, cucumber and onion. For an extra special touch, add a little crushed ice to the garnish.

Split Pea and Ham Soup

The main ingredient for this dish is bacon hock, which is the narrow piece of bone cut from a leg of ham. You could use a piece of pork belly instead, if you prefer, and remove it with the herbs before serving.

INGREDIENTS

Serves 4

450g/1lb/2½ cups green split peas

4 rindless bacon rashers (strips)

1 onion, coarsely chopped

2 carrots, sliced

1 celery stick, sliced

2.4 litres/4¼ pints/10½ cups water

1 fresh thyme sprig

2 bay leaves

1 large potato, coarsely diced

1 bacon hock

ground black pepper

1 Put the split peas into a bowl, cover with cold water and leave to soak overnight.

2 Cut the bacon rashers into small pieces. In a large pan, dry-fry the bacon for 4–5 minutes. or until crisp. Remove from the pan with a slotted spoon.

3 Add the chopped onion, carrots and celery to the fat in the pan and cook for 3–4 minutes, until the onion is softened but not brown. Return the diced bacon to the pan with the water.

4 Drain the split peas and add to the pan with the thyme, bay leaves, potato and bacon hock. Bring to the boil, reduce the heat, cover and cook gently for 1 hour.

5 Remove the thyme, bay leaves and hock. Process the soup in a blender or food processor until smooth. Return to a clean pan. Cut the meat from the hock and add to the soup and heat through gently. Season with plenty of ground black pepper. Ladle into warm soup bowls and serve immediately.

Summer Tomato Soup

The success of this soup depends on having ripe, full-flavoured tomatoes, such as the oval plum variety, so make it when the tomato season is at its peak.

INGREDIENTS

Serves 4

15ml/1 tbsp olive oil

1 large onion, chopped

1 carrot, chopped

1kg/2¼lb ripe tomatoes, quartered

2 garlic cloves, chopped

5 fresh thyme sprigs, or
  1.5ml/¼ tsp dried thyme

4–5 fresh marjoram sprigs, or
  1.5ml/¼ tsp dried marjoram

1 bay leaf

45ml/3 tbsp crème fraîche, sour cream or
  natural (plain) yogurt, plus a little extra
  to garnish

salt and ground black pepper

1 Heat the olive oil in a large, preferably stainless steel pan or flameproof casserole.

2 Add the onion and carrot and cook for 3–4 minutes.

3 Add the quartered tomatoes, chopped garlic and herbs. Reduce the heat and simmer, covered, for 30 minutes.

4 Discard the bay leaf and pass the soup through a food mill or press through a sieve. Leave to cool, then chill in the refrigerator.

VARIATION

If you like, you can use oregano instead of marjoram, and parsley instead of thyme.

MEAT &
POULTRY
SOUPS

Miami Avocado Soup

Avocados are combined with lemon juice, dry sherry and an optional dash of hot pepper sauce, to make this subtle chilled soup.

INGREDIENTS

Serves 4

2 large or 3 medium ripe avocados

15ml/1 tbsp fresh lemon juice

75g/3oz/¾ cup coarsely chopped
   peeled cucumber

30ml/2 tbsp dry sherry

25g/1oz/¼ cup coarsely chopped spring
   onions (scallions), with some of the
   green stems

475ml/16fl oz/2 cups Chicken Stock

5ml/1 tsp salt

hot pepper sauce (optional)

natural (plain) yogurt, to garnish

1 Cut the avocados in half, remove the stones (pits) and peel. Coarsely chop the flesh and place in a food processor or blender. Add the lemon juice and process until very smooth.

2 Add the cucumber, sherry and most of the spring onions, reserving a few for the garnish. Process again until smooth.

3 In a large bowl, combine the avocado mixture with the chicken stock. Whisk until well blended. Season with the salt and a few drops of hot pepper sauce, if you like. Cover the bowl with clear film (plastic wrap) and place in the refrigerator to chill thoroughly.

4 To serve, fill four individual bowls with the soup. Place a spoonful of yogurt in the centre of each bowl and swirl with a spoon. Finally, sprinkle with the reserved chopped spring onions.

Pumpkin and Coconut Soup

Rich and sweet flavours are married beautifully with sharp and hot in this creamy South-east Asian-influenced soup.

INGREDIENTS

Serves 4–6

2 garlic cloves, crushed

4 shallots, finely crushed

2.5ml/½ tsp shrimp paste

15ml/1 tbsp dried shrimp, soaked
   for 10 minutes and drained

1 lemon grass stalk, chopped

2 fresh green chillies, seeded

600ml/1 pint/2½ cups Chicken Stock

450g/1lb pumpkin, cut into thick chunks

600ml/1 pint/2½ cups coconut cream

30ml/2 tbsp Thai fish sauce

5ml/1 tsp sugar

115g/4oz cooked peeled prawns (shrimp)

salt and ground black pepper

For the garnish

2 fresh red chillies, seeded and
   thinly sliced

10–12 fresh basil leaves

1 Using a mortar and pestle, grind the garlic, shallots, shrimp paste, dried shrimp, lemon grass, green chillies and a pinch of salt into a paste.

2 Bring the chicken stock to the boil in a large, add the paste and stir until dissolved.

3 Lower the heat, add the chunks of pumpkin, and simmer for about 10–15 minutes, or until the pumpkin is tender.

4 Stir in the coconut cream, then bring back to a simmer. Add the fish sauce, sugar and ground black pepper to taste.

5 Add the prawns and cook until they are heated through. Serve garnished with the sliced red chillies and basil leaves.

COOK'S TIP

Shrimp paste, which is made from ground shrimp fermented in brine, is used to give food a savoury flavour.

CREAMED
VEGETABLE
SOUPS

Spinach and Tofu Soup

This is an extremely delicate and mild-flavoured soup, which can be used to counterbalance the heat from a hot Thai curry to follow.

INGREDIENTS

Serves 4–6

30ml/2 tbsp dried shrimp

1 litre/1¾ pints/4 cups Chicken Stock

225g/8oz fresh tofu, drained and cut into
    2cm/¾in cubes

30ml/2 tbsp Thai fish sauce

350g/12oz fresh spinach

ground black pepper

2 spring onions (scallions), thinly sliced,
    to garnish

1 Rinse and drain the dried shrimp. Combine the shrimp with the chicken stock in a large pan and bring to the boil. Add the tofu and simmer for about 5 minutes. Season with fish sauce and black pepper to taste.

2 Wash the spinach leaves and tear into bitesize pieces. Add to the soup and cook for another 1–2 minutes.

3 Pour the soup into warmed bowls, sprinkle the chopped spring onions on top and serve.

Italian Tomato Soup

This is the perfect soup for late summer when fresh tomatoes are at their most flavoursome.

INGREDIENTS

Serves 4–6

15ml/1 tbsp olive oil

25g/1oz/2 tbsp butter

1 onion, finely chopped

900g/2lb ripe Italian plum tomatoes, coarsely chopped

1 garlic clove, coarsely chopped

750ml/1¼ pints/3 cups Chicken Stock

120ml/4 fl oz/½ cup dry white wine

30ml/2 tbsp sun-dried tomato paste

30ml/2 tbsp shredded fresh basil, plus a few whole leaves to garnish

150ml/¼ pint/⅔ cup double (heavy) cream

salt and ground black pepper

1 Heat the oil and butter in a large pan until foaming. Add the onion and cook gently, stirring frequently, for about 5 minutes, until softened, but not brown.

2 Stir in the chopped tomatoes and garlic, then add the stock, white wine and sun-dried tomato paste and season with salt and pepper to taste.

3 Bring to the boil, then lower the heat, half-cover the pan and simmer gently for 20 minutes, stirring occasionally to stop the tomatoes from sticking to the base of the pan.

4 Process the soup with the shredded basil in a food processor or blender, then press through a sieve into a clean pan.

5 Add the double cream and heat through, stirring. Do not allow the soup to approach boiling point. Check the consistency and add more stock, if necessary. Adjust the seasoning to taste, pour the soup into heated bowls and garnish with whole basil leaves. Serve immediately.

Thai Fish Soup

Thai fish sauce, or nam pla, *is rich in B vitamins and is used extensively in Thai cooking. It is available at Thai or Indonesian stores and good supermarkets.*

INGREDIENTS

Serves 4

350g/12oz raw large prawns (shrimp)
15ml/1 tbsp groundnut (peanut) oil
1.2 litres/2 pints/5 cups Chicken or
    Fish Stock
1 lemon grass stalk, bruised and cut into
    2.5cm/1in lengths
2 kaffir lime leaves, torn into pieces
juice and finely grated rind of 1 lime
½ fresh green chilli, seeded and
    thinly sliced
4 scallops
24 fresh mussels, scrubbed and debearded
115g/4oz monkfish fillet, cut into
    2cm/¾in chunks
10ml/2 tsp Thai fish sauce

For the garnish
1 kaffir lime leaf, shredded
½ fresh red chilli, thinly sliced

1 Peel the prawns, reserving the shells, and remove the black vein running along their backs.

2 Heat the oil in a pan and fry the prawn shells until pink. Add the stock, lemon grass, lime leaves, lime rind and green chilli. Bring to the boil, simmer for 20 minutes, then strain through a sieve, reserving the liquid.

3 Cut the scallops in half, leaving the corals attached.

4 Return the stock to a clean pan, add the prawns, mussels, monkfish and scallops and cook for 3 minutes. Remove from the heat and add the lime juice and fish sauce.

5 Serve immediately, garnished with the shredded lime leaf and thinly sliced red chilli.

Fish & Shellfish Soups

Wild Mushroom Soup

Wild mushrooms are expensive. Dried porcini have an intense flavour, so only a small quantity is needed. Meat stock may seem odd in a vegetable soup, but it helps to strengthen the earthy flavour.

INGREDIENTS

Serves 4

25g/1oz/2 cups dried porcini mushrooms

250ml/8fl oz/1 cup warm water

30ml/2 tbsp olive oil

15g/¹/₂oz/1 tbsp butter

2 leeks, thinly sliced

2 shallots, coarsely chopped

1 garlic clove, coarsely chopped

225g/8oz fresh wild mushrooms

1.2 litres/2 pints/5 cups Meat Stock

2.5ml/¹/₂ tsp dried thyme

150ml/¹/₄ pint/²/₃ cup double (heavy) cream

salt and ground black pepper

fresh thyme sprigs, to garnish

3 Chop or thinly slice the fresh mushrooms and add to the pan. Stir over a medium heat for a few minutes until they begin to soften. Pour in the meat stock and bring to the boil. Add the porcini, soaking liquid, dried thyme and salt and pepper. Lower the heat, half-cover the pan and simmer gently for 30 minutes, stirring occasionally.

4 Pour about three-quarters of the soup into a blender or food processor and process until smooth. Return to the soup remaining in the pan, stir in the double cream and heat through. Check the consistency, adding more stock or water if the soup is too thick. Taste and adjust the seasoning. Serve hot, garnished with sprigs of fresh thyme.

1 Put the dried porcini in a bowl, add the warm water and leave to soak for 20–30 minutes. Lift out of the liquid and squeeze to remove as much of the soaking liquid as possible. Strain all the liquid and reserve to use later. Finely chop the porcini.

2 Heat the oil and butter in a large pan until foaming. Add the leeks, shallots and garlic and cook gently for about 5 minutes, stirring frequently, until softened but not coloured.

Creamed Vegetable Soups

Malayan Prawn Laksa

This spicy prawn and noodle soup tastes just as good when made with fresh crab meat or any flaked cooked fish. If you are short of time or can't find all the spice paste ingredients, buy ready-made laksa paste, which is available from Asian stores.

INGREDIENTS

Serves 3–4

115g/4oz rice vermicelli or stir-fry
   rice noodles
15ml/1 tbsp vegetable oil
600ml/1 pint/2½ cups Fish Stock
400ml/14fl oz/1⅔ cups thin coconut milk
30ml/2 tbsp Thai fish sauce
½ lime
16–24 cooked peeled prawns (shrimp)
salt and cayenne pepper
60ml/4 tbsp fresh coriander (cilantro)
   sprigs and leaves, chopped, to garnish

For the spice paste
2 lemon grass stalks, finely chopped
2 fresh red chillies, seeded and chopped
2.5cm/1in piece fresh root
   ginger, sliced
2.5ml/½ tsp shrimp paste
2 garlic cloves, chopped
2.5ml/½ tsp ground turmeric
30ml/2 tbsp tamarind paste

1 Cook the rice vermicelli or noodles in a large pan of salted, boiling water according to the instructions on the packet. Tip into a large sieve or colander, then rinse under cold water and drain. Set aside on a warm plate.

2 To make the spice paste, place all the ingredients in a mortar and pound with a pestle. Or, if you prefer, put the ingredients in a food processor or blender and then process until a smooth paste is formed.

3 Heat the oil in a large pan, add the spice paste and fry, stirring constantly, for a few moments to release all the flavours, but be careful not to let it burn.

4 Add the fish stock and coconut milk and bring to the boil. Stir in the fish sauce, then simmer for 5 minutes. Season with salt and cayenne to taste, adding a squeeze of lime. Add the prawns and heat through for a few seconds.

5 Divide the noodles among three or four soup plates. Pour the soup over, making sure that each portion includes an equal number of prawns. Garnish with coriander and serve piping hot.

Cream of Tomato Soup

Tomato soup is an old favourite. This version is made special by the addition of fresh herbs and cream.

INGREDIENTS

Serves 4

25g/1oz/2 tbsp butter or margarine

1 onion, chopped

900g/2lb tomatoes, peeled and quartered

2 carrots, chopped

450ml/¾ pint/scant 2 cups Chicken Stock

30ml/2 tbsp chopped fresh parsley

2.5ml/½ tsp fresh thyme leaves, plus extra
   to garnish

75ml/5 tbsp whipping cream

salt and ground black pepper

1 Melt the butter or margarine in a large, heavy pan. Add the onion and cook for 5 minutes, until softened.

2 Stir in the tomato quarters, carrots, chicken stock, parsley and thyme. Bring to the boil, then reduce the heat to low, cover the pan and simmer gently for about 15–20 minutes, until all the vegetables are tender.

3 Purée the soup in a vegetable mill until it is smooth. Alternatively, process the soup in a blender or food processor, then press through a sieve. Return the puréed soup to the pan.

4 Stir in the cream and reheat gently. Season the soup to taste with salt and ground black pepper. Ladle into warmed soup bowls and serve immediately while piping hot, garnished with fresh thyme leaves.

COOK'S TIP

Meaty and flavourful, Italian plum tomatoes are the best choice for this soup.

Hot and Sour Prawn Soup with Lemon Grass

This classic seafood soup, known as
Tom Yam Goong, *is probably the*
most popular and best-known soup
from Thailand.

INGREDIENTS

Serves 4–6

450 g/1 lb king prawns (jumbo shrimp)

1 litre/1¾ pints/4 cups chicken stock
 or water

3 lemon grass stalks

10 kaffir lime leaves, torn in half

225 g/8 oz can straw mushrooms, drained

45 ml/3 tbsp fish sauce

50 ml/2 fl oz/¼ cup lime juice

30 ml/2 tbsp chopped spring onion (scallion)

15 ml/1 tbsp fresh coriander (cilantro) leaves

4 fresh red chillies, seeded and chopped

2 spring onions (scallions), finely
 chopped, to garnish

1 Shell and devein the prawns
and set aside. Rinse the prawn
shells and place in a large pan
with the stock or water and bring
to the boil.

2 Bruise the lemon grass stalks
with the blunt edge of a
chopping knife and add them to
the stock, together with half the
lime leaves. Simmer gently for
5–6 minutes until the stalks change
colour and the stock is fragrant.

3 Strain the stock, return to the
pan and reheat. Add the
mushrooms and prawns, then
cook until the prawns turn pink.

4 Stir in the fish sauce, lime
juice, spring onion, coriander,
red chillies and the rest of the lime
leaves. Taste and adjust the
seasoning. The soup should be
sour, salty, spicy and hot. Garnish
with finely chopped spring onions
before serving.

Cream of Spring Onion Soup

The oniony flavour of this soup is surprisingly delicate.

INGREDIENTS

Serves 4–6

25g/1oz/2 tbsp butter
1 small onion, chopped
bunch of spring onions (scallions), chopped
225g/8oz potatoes, chopped
600ml/1 pint/2½ cups Vegetable Stock
350ml/12fl oz/1½ cups single
   (light) cream
30ml/2 tbsp lemon juice
salt and freshly ground white pepper
chopped fresh chives, to garnish

1 Melt the butter in a pan and add all the onions. Cover and cook over very low heat for about 10 minutes or until soft.

2 Add the potatoes and the stock. Bring to the boil, then cover again and simmer over a moderately low heat for about 30 minutes. Cool slightly.

3 Process the soup in a blender or food processor.

4 If serving the soup hot, pour it back into the pan. Add the cream and season to taste with salt and pepper. Reheat the soup gently, stirring occasionally. Add the lemon juice.

5 If serving the soup cold, pour it into a bowl. Stir in the cream and lemon juice and season with salt and pepper. Cover the bowl and chill for at least 1 hour.

6 Sprinkle with the chopped fresh chives before serving, whether hot or chilled.

Fish Ball Soup

The Japanese name for this soup is Tsumire-jiru. Tsumire *means, quite literally, sardine balls, and these are added to this delicious soup to impart their robust flavour.*

INGREDIENTS

Serves 4

100ml/3½fl oz/generous ⅓ cup sake or
   dry white wine
1.2 litres/2 pints/5 cups instant dashi
60ml/4 tbsp white miso paste

For the fish balls

20g/¾oz fresh root ginger
800g/1¾lb fresh sardines, gutted and
   heads removed
30ml/2 tbsp white miso paste
15ml/1 tbsp sake or dry white wine
7.5ml/1½ tsp sugar
1 egg
30ml/2 tbsp cornflour (cornstarch)
150g/5 oz shimeji mushrooms or
   6 shiitake mushrooms
1 leek or large spring onion (scallion)

1 First make the fish balls. To do this, grate the ginger and squeeze it well to yield 5ml/1 tsp ginger juice.

2 Rinse the sardines under cold running water, then cut them in half along the backbones. Remove and discard all the bones. To skin a boned sardine, lay it skin side down on a board, then run a sharp knife slowly along the skin from tail to head.

3 Coarsely chop the sardines and process with the ginger juice, miso, sake or wine, sugar and egg to a thick paste in a food processor or blender. Transfer to a bowl and mix in the cornflour until thoroughly blended.

4 Trim the shimeji mushrooms and either separate each stem or remove the stems from the shiitake mushrooms and shred them. Cut the leek or spring onion into 4cm/1½in strips.

5 Bring the ingredients for the soup to the boil. Use 2 wet spoons to shape small portions of the sardine mixture into bitesize balls and drop them into the soup. Add the prepared mushrooms and leek or spring onion.

6 Gently simmer the soup until the sardine balls float to the surface. Serve immediately, in individual, deep soup bowls.

Butternut Squash Bisque

This is a fragrant, creamy and delicately flavoured soup.

INGREDIENTS

Serves 4

25g/1oz/2 tbsp butter or margarine

2 small onions, finely chopped

450g/1lb butternut squash, peeled, seeded and cubed

1.2 litres/2 pints/5 cups Chicken Stock

225g/8oz potatoes, cubed

5ml/1 tsp paprika

120ml/4fl oz/½ cup whipping cream (optional)

25ml/1½ tbsp chopped fresh chives, plus a few whole chives to garnish

salt and ground black pepper

1 Melt the butter or margarine in a large pan. Add the onions and cook over a medium heat for about 5 minutes, until soft.

2 Add the squash, chicken stock, potatoes and paprika. Bring to the boil. Reduce the heat to low, cover the pan and simmer gently for about 35 minutes until all the vegetables are soft.

3 Pour the soup into a food processor or blender and process until smooth. Return the soup to the pan and stir in the cream, if using. Season with salt and pepper. Reheat gently.

4 Stir in the chopped chives just before serving. Garnish each serving with a few whole chives and serve hot.

Prawn Creole

Raw prawns are combined with chopped fresh vegetables and cayenne pepper to make this tasty soup.

INGREDIENTS

Serves 4

675g/1½lb raw prawns (shrimp) in the shell, with heads, if available

475ml/16fl oz/2 cups water

45ml/3 tbsp olive or vegetable oil

175g/6oz/1½ cups very finely chopped onions

75g/3oz/½ cup very finely chopped celery

75g/3oz/½ cup very finely chopped green (bell) pepper

25g/1oz/½ cup chopped fresh parsley

1 garlic clove, crushed

15ml/1 tbsp Worcestershire sauce

1.5ml/¼ tsp cayenne pepper

120ml/4fl oz/½ cup dry white wine

50g/2oz/1 cup chopped peeled plum tomatoes

5ml/1 tsp salt

1 bay leaf

5ml/1 tsp sugar

fresh parsley, to garnish

boiled rice, to serve

1 Peel and devein the prawns, reserving the heads and shells. Keep the prawns in a covered bowl in the refrigerator while you make the soup.

2 Put the prawn heads and shells in a pan with the water. Bring to the boil and simmer for 15 minutes. Strain, then measure 350ml/12fl oz/1½ cups of the stock and reserve.

3 Heat the oil in a heavy pan. Add the onions and cook over a low heat for 8–10 minutes, until softened. Add the celery and green pepper and cook for 5 minutes more. Stir in the parsley, garlic, Worcestershire sauce and cayenne. Cook for a further 5 minutes.

4 Raise the heat to medium. Stir in the wine and simmer for 3–4 minutes. Add the tomatoes, reserved prawn stock, salt, bay leaf and sugar and bring to the boil. Stir well, then reduce the heat to low and simmer for about 30 minutes, until the tomatoes have fallen apart and the sauce has reduced slightly. Remove from the heat and cool slightly.

5 Discard the bay leaf. Pour the sauce into a food processor or blender and process until quite smooth. Taste and adjust the seasoning as necessary.

6 Return the tomato soup to the pan and bring to the boil. Add the prawns and simmer for 4–5 minutes, until they turn pink. Ladle into warm individual soup bowls, garnish with fresh parsley and serve with rice.

Cream of Red Pepper Soup

Grilling peppers gives them a sweet, smoky flavour, which is delicious in salads or, as here, in a velvety soup with a secret flavouring of rosemary to add aromatic depth. The soup is equally good served hot or chilled, as you prefer.

INGREDIENTS

Serves 4

4 red (bell) peppers
25g/1oz/2 tbsp butter
1 onion, finely chopped
1 fresh rosemary sprig
1.2 litres/2 pints/5 cups Chicken or
    Vegetable Stock
45ml/3 tbsp tomato purée (paste)
120ml/4fl oz/½ cup double (heavy) cream
paprika
salt and ground black pepper

1 Preheat the grill (broiler). Put the peppers in the grill pan under the grill and turn them regularly until the skins have blackened all around. Put them into plastic bags, sealing them closed. Leave them for 20 minutes.

2 Peel the blackened skin off the peppers. If possible, avoid rinsing them under running water, as this loses some of the natural oil and hence the flavour.

3 Halve the peppers, removing the seeds, stalks and pith, then coarsely chop the flesh.

4 Melt the butter in a deep pan. Add the onion and rosemary and cook gently over a low heat for about 5 minutes. Remove the rosemary and discard.

5 Add the peppers and stock to the onion, bring to the boil and simmer for 15 minutes. Stir in the tomato purée, then process or sieve the soup to a smooth purée.

6 Stir in half the cream and season with paprika, salt, if necessary, and pepper.

7 Serve the soup hot or chilled, with the remaining cream swirled delicately on top. Speckle the cream very lightly with a pinch of paprika.

Fish and Sweet Potato Soup

The subtle sweetness of the potato, combined with the fish and the aromatic flavour of oregano, makes this an appetizing soup.

INGREDIENTS

Serves 4

½ onion, chopped

175g/6oz sweet potato, peeled and diced

175g/6oz white fish fillet, skinned

50g/2oz carrot, chopped

5ml/1 tsp chopped fresh oregano or
  2.5ml/½ tsp dried oregano

2.5ml/½ tsp ground cinnamon

1.5 litres/2½ pints/6¼ cups Fish Stock

75ml/5 tbsp single (light) cream

chopped fresh parsley, to garnish

1 Put the chopped onion, diced sweet potato, white fish, chopped carrot, oregano, cinnamon and half of the fish stock in a pan. Bring to the boil, then lower the heat and simmer for 20 minutes, or until the potato is cooked.

2 Leave to cool, then pour into a blender or food processor and process until smooth.

3 Return the soup to the pan, then add the remaining fish stock and gradually bring to the boil. Reduce the heat to low and add the single cream, then gently heat through, without boiling, stirring occasionally.

4 Serve hot in warmed soup bowls, garnished with the chopped fresh parsley.

VARIATION

Garnish with chopped fresh tarragon instead of parsley.

Yogurt Soup

Some communities in India add sugar to this soup.

INGREDIENTS

Serves 4–6

450ml/¾ pint/scant 2 cups natural (plain) yogurt, beaten

25g/1oz/¼ cup gram flour (besan)

2.5ml/½ tsp chilli powder

2.5ml/½ tsp turmeric salt, to taste

2–3 fresh green chillies, finely chopped

60ml/4 tbsp vegetable oil

1 dried red chilli

5ml/1 tsp cumin seeds

3–4 curry leaves

3 garlic cloves, crushed

5cm/2in piece fresh root ginger, crushed

30ml/2 tbsp chopped fresh coriander (cilantro)

1 Mix together the yogurt, flour, chilli powder and turmeric salt and pass through a strainer into a pan. Add the fresh green chillies and cook gently for about 10 minutes, stirring occasionally. Be careful not to let the soup boil over.

2 Heat the oil in a frying pan and fry the dried chilli, cumin seeds, curry leaves, garlic and ginger until the dried chilli turns black. Stir in 15ml/1 tbsp of the chopped fresh coriander.

3 Pour the spices over the yogurt soup, cover the pan and leave to rest for 5 minutes. Mix well and gently reheat for 5 minutes more. Serve hot, garnished with the remaining chopped coriander.

Smoked Cod and Okra Soup

The inspiration for this soup came from a Ghanaian recipe for okra soup. Here it is enhanced by the addition of smoked fish.

INGREDIENTS

Serves 4

2 green bananas

50g/2oz/¼ cup butter or margarine

1 onion, finely chopped

2 tomatoes, peeled and finely chopped

115g/4oz okra, trimmed

225g/8oz smoked cod fillet, cut into
    bitesize pieces

900ml/1½ pints/3¾ cups Fish Stock

1 fresh chilli, seeded and chopped

salt and ground black pepper

fresh parsley sprigs, to garnish

3 Add the cod, fish stock, chilli and seasoning. Bring to the boil, then reduce the heat and simmer for about 20 minutes, or until the cod is cooked through and flakes easily.

4 Peel the cooked bananas and cut into slices. Stir into the soup, heat through for a few minutes and ladle into warm soup bowls. Garnish with parsley and serve immediately.

1 Slit the skins of the green bananas and place in a large pan. Cover with water, bring to the boil and cook over a moderate heat for 25 minutes, until the bananas are tender. Transfer to a plate and leave to cool.

2 Melt the butter or margarine in a large pan and cook the onion for about 5 minutes, until soft. Stir in the chopped tomatoes and okra and cook gently for a further 10 minutes.

Broccoli and Stilton Soup

This is a really easy, but rich soup –
choose something simple to follow,
such as plainly roasted or grilled
meat, poultry or fish.

Serves 4

350g/12oz broccoli

25g/1oz/2 tbsp butter

1 onion, chopped

1 leek, white part only, chopped

1 small potato, cut into chunks

600ml/1 pint/2½ cups hot Chicken Stock

300ml/½ pint/1¼ cups milk

45ml/3 tbsp double (heavy) cream

115g/4 oz Stilton cheese, rind
rcmoved, crumbled

salt and ground black pepper

1 Break the broccoli into florets,
discarding any tough stems.
Set aside two small florets to
garnish the finished dish.

2 Melt the butter in a large pan
and cook the onion and leek
until soft, but not coloured. Add
the broccoli and potato, then pour
in the stock. Cover and simmer for
15–20 minutes, until the vegetables
are tender.

3 Cool slightly then pour into a
blender or food processor and
process until smooth. Strain the
mixture through a sieve back into
the rinsed pan.

4 Add the milk and double
cream to the pan. Season to
taste with salt and ground black
pepper. Reheat gently. At the last
minute, add the cheese, stirring
until it just melts. Do not boil.

5 Meanwhile, blanch the
reserved broccoli florets and
cut them vertically into thin slices.
Ladle the soup into warmed bowls
and garnish with the sliced
broccoli and a generous grinding
of black pepper.

Creamed Vegetable Soups

Creamy Fish Chowder

A traditional soup that never fails to please, whether it is made with milk or more luxuriously, with a generous quantity of cream.

INGREDIENTS

Serves 4

3 thick-cut bacon rashers (strips)
1 large onion
675g/1½lb potatoes
1 litre/1¾ pints/4 cups Fish Stock
450g/1lb skinless haddock, cut into
    2.5cm/1in cubes
30ml/2 tbsp chopped fresh parsley
15ml/1 tbsp chopped fresh chives
300ml/½ pint/1¼ cups whipping cream
    or milk
salt and ground black pepper

1 Remove the rind from the bacon and discard it; cut the bacon into small pieces. Chop the onion and cut the potatoes into 2cm/¾in cubes.

2 Fry the bacon in a deep pan until the fat is rendered. Add the onion and potatoes and cook over a low heat, without browning, for about 10 minutes. Season to taste with salt and pepper.

3 Pour off the excess bacon fat from the pan. Add the fish stock to the pan and bring to a boil. Lower the heat and simmer for about 15–20 minutes, until the vegetables are tender.

4 Gently stir in the cubes of haddock, the parsley and chives. Simmer for 3–4 minutes, until the fish is just cooked.

5 Stir the cream or milk into the chowder and reheat gently, but do not bring to the boil. Taste and adjust the seasoning if necessary and serve immediately.

VARIATION
❧

Cod fillets would be equally good in this chowder, or try smoked fillets for a stronger taste.

Fresh Pea Soup St Germain

This soup takes its name from a suburb of Paris where peas used to be cultivated in market gardens.

INGREDIENTS

INGREDIENTS

Serves 2–3

small knob (pat) of butter

2–3 shallots, finely chopped

400g/14oz/3 cups shelled fresh peas (from about 1.5kg/3lb garden peas)

500ml/17fl oz/2¼ cups water

45–60ml/3–4 tbsp whipping cream (optional)

salt and ground black pepper

Crispy Croûtons, to garnish

3 When the peas are tender, ladle them into a blender or food processor with a little of the cooking liquid and process until completely smooth.

4 Strain the soup into the pan or casserole, stir in the cream, if using, and heat through without boiling. Add the seasoning and serve hot, garnished with croûtons.

COOK'S TIP

If fresh peas are not available, use frozen peas, but thaw and rinse them before use.

1 Melt the butter in a heavy pan or flameproof casserole. Add the shallots and cook over a medium heat for about 3 minutes, stirring occasionally.

2 Add the peas and water and season with salt and a little pepper. Cover and simmer for about 12 minutes for young peas and up to 18 minutes for large or older peas, stirring occasionally.

Corn and Scallop Chowder

Fresh corn is ideal for this chowder, although canned or frozen corn also works well.

INGREDIENTS

Serves 4–6

2 corn cobs or 200g/7 oz/generous
   1 cup frozen or canned corn kernels

600ml/1 pint/2½ cups milk

15g/½oz/1 tbsp butter or margarine

1 small leek or onion, chopped

40g/1½oz/¼ cup smoked streaky (fatty)
   bacon, finely chopped

1 small garlic clove, crushed

1 small green (bell) pepper, seeded
   and diced

1 celery stick, chopped

1 potato, diced

15ml/1 tbsp plain (all-
   purpose) flour

300ml/½ pint/1¼ cups Chicken or
   Vegetable stock

4 scallops

115g/4 oz cooked fresh mussels

pinch of paprika

150ml/¼ pint/⅔ cup single (light)
   cream (optional)

salt and ground black pepper

1 If using fresh corn cobs, slice down them with a sharp knife to remove the kernels. If using canned corn kernels, drain well. Place half the kernels in a food processor or blender and process with a little of the milk. Set the other half aside.

2 Melt the butter or margarine in a large pan and cook the leek or onion, bacon and garlic over a low heat, stirring frequently, for 4–5 minutes, until the leek is soft, but not browned.

3 Add the green pepper, celery and potato and sweat over a gentle heat for 3–4 minutes more, stirring frequently.

4 Stir in the flour and cook for about 1–2 minutes, until golden and frothy. Stir in a little milk and the corn mixture, stock, the remaining milk and corn kernels and seasoning.

5 Bring to the boil, and then simmer, partially covered, for 15–20 minutes, until the vegetables are tender.

6 Pull the corals away from the scallops and slice the white flesh into 5mm/¼in slices. Stir the scallops into the soup, cook for 4 minutes and then stir in the corals, mussels and paprika. Heat through for a few minutes and then stir in the cream, if using. Check the seasoning and serve.

Green Bean and Parmesan Soup

Fresh green beans and Parmesan cheese make a simple, but delicious combination of flavours.

INGREDIENTS

Serves 4

25g/1oz/2 tbsp butter or margarine

225g/8oz green beans, trimmed

1 garlic clove, crushed

450ml/¾ pint/scant 2 cups
   Vegetable Stock

40g/1½oz/½ cup grated Parmesan cheese

50ml/2fl oz/¼ cup single (light) cream

salt and ground black pepper

30ml/2 tbsp chopped fresh parsley,
   to garnish

1 Melt the butter or margarine in a medium pan. Add the green beans and garlic and cook for 2–3 minutes over a medium heat, stirring frequently.

2 Stir in the stock and season with salt and pepper. Bring to the boil, then simmer, uncovered, for 10–15 minutes, until the beans are tender.

3 Pour the soup into a blender or food processor and process until smooth. Alternatively, purée the soup in a food mill. Return to the pan and reheat gently.

4 Stir in the Parmesan and cream. Sprinkle with the parsley and serve immediately.

Clam and Basil Soup

Subtly sweet and spicy, this soup is an ideal first course for serving as part of a celebration dinner.

INGREDIENTS

Serves 4–6

30ml/2 tbsp olive oil

1 onion, finely chopped

leaves from 1 fresh or dried sprig of
  thyme, chopped or crumbled

2 garlic cloves, crushed

5–6 fresh basil leaves, plus extra to garnish

1.5–2.5ml/¼–½ tsp crushed red chillies,
  to taste

1 litre/1¾ pints/4 cups Fish Stock

350ml/12fl oz/1½ cups passata (bottled
  strained tomatoes)

5ml/1 tsp granulated sugar

90g/3½oz/scant 1 cup frozen peas

65g/2½oz/⅔ cup small dried pasta
  shapes, such as chifferini

225g/8oz frozen shelled clams

salt and ground black pepper

1 Heat the oil in a large pan, add the onion and cook gently for about 5 minutes, until softened, but not coloured. Add the thyme, then stir in the garlic, basil leaves and chillies.

2 Add the stock, passata and sugar to the pan and season with salt and pepper to taste. Bring to the boil, then lower the heat and simmer gently for 15 minutes, stirring occasionally. Add the frozen peas and cook for a further 5 minutes.

3 Add the pasta to the stock mixture and bring to the boil, stirring constantly. Lower the heat and simmer for about 5 minutes, or according to the packet instructions, stirring frequently, until the pasta is *al dente*.

4 Turn the heat down to low, add the frozen clams and heat through for 2–3 minutes. Taste and adjust the seasoning if necessary. Serve immediately in warmed bowls, garnished with basil leaves.

COOK'S TIP

Frozen shelled clams are available at good fishmongers and supermarkets. If you can't get them, use bottled or canned clams in natural juice (not vinegar). Italian delicatessens sell jars of clams in their shells. These both look and taste delicious and are not too expensive. For a special occasion, stir some into the soup.

Cream of Spinach Soup

*This is a deliciously creamy soup
that you will make again and again.*

INGREDIENTS

Serves 4

25g/1oz/2 tbsp butter

1 small onion, chopped

675g/1½lb fresh spinach, chopped

1.2 litres/2 pints/5 cups Vegetable Stock

50g/2 oz creamed coconut or

    250ml/8fl oz/1 cup coconut cream

freshly grated nutmeg

300ml/½ pint/1¼ cups whipping cream

salt and ground black pepper

long strips of fresh chives, to garnish

3 Return the mixture to the pan
and add the remaining stock
and the coconut, with salt, pepper
and nutmeg to taste. Simmer for
15 minutes to thicken.

4 Add the cream to the pan,
stir well and heat through, but
do not allow the soup to boil. Serve
immediately, garnished with long
strips of chives.

1 Melt the butter in a pan over a
moderate heat and sauté the
onion, stirring occasionally, for a
few minutes until soft. Add the
spinach, cover the pan and cook
gently for 10 minutes, until the
spinach has wilted and reduced.

2 Pour the spinach mixture into
a blender or food processor
and add a little of the stock. Blend
until smooth.

Creamed Vegetable Soups

Saffron Mussel Soup

This is one of France's most delicious seafood soups. For everyday eating, the French would normally serve all the mussels in their shells. Serve with plenty of French bread.

INGREDIENTS

Serves 4–6

40g/1½oz/3 tbsp unsalted (sweet) butter

8 shallots, finely chopped

1 bouquet garni

5ml/1 tsp black peppercorns

350ml/12fl oz/1½ cups dry white wine

1kg/2¼lb fresh mussels, scrubbed
   and debearded

2 leeks, trimmed and finely chopped

1 fennel bulb, finely chopped

1 carrot, finely chopped

several saffron threads

1 litre/1¾ pints/4 cups Fish or
   Chicken Stock

30–45ml/2–3 tbsp cornflour (cornstarch),
   blended with 45ml/3 tbsp cold water

120ml/4fl oz/½ cup whipping cream

1 tomato, peeled, seeded and
   finely chopped

30ml/2 tbsp Pernod (optional)

salt and ground black pepper

1 In a large, heavy pan, melt half the butter over a medium-high heat. Add half the shallots and cook, stirring frequently, for 1–2 minutes, until softened but not coloured. Add the bouquet garni, peppercorns and white wine and bring to the boil. Add the mussels, cover tightly with a lid and cook over a high heat for 3–5 minutes, shaking the pan occasionally, until the mussel shells have opened.

2 With a slotted spoon, transfer the mussels to a bowl and set aside. Strain the cooking liquid through a sieve lined with muslin (cheesecloth) to remove any sand or grit and reserve.

3 Pull open the shells and remove most of the mussels. Discard any closed mussels.

4 Melt the remaining butter over a medium heat. Add the remaining shallots and cook for 1–2 minutes. Add the leeks, fennel, carrot and saffron and cook for 3–5 minutes.

5 Stir in the reserved cooking liquid, bring to the boil and cook for 5 minutes, until the vegetables are tender and the liquid is slightly reduced. Add the stock and bring to the boil, skimming any foam that rises to the surface. Season with salt, if needed, and black pepper and cook for a further 5 minutes.

6 Stir the blended cornflour into the soup. Simmer, stirring constantly, for 2–3 minutes, until the soup is slightly thickened, then stir in the cream, mussels and chopped tomato. Add the Pernod, if using, and cook for 1–2 minutes, until hot, then ladle into warm bowls and serve immediately.

Cream of Leek and Potato Soup

Serve this flavourful soup with a spoonful of crème fraîche or sour cream and sprinkle with a few chopped fresh chives – or, for special occasions, with a spoonful of caviar.

INGREDIENTS

Serves 6–8

450g/1lb potatoes, peeled and cubed

1.5 litres/2½ pints/6¼ cups Chicken
　　Stock

350g/12 oz leeks, trimmed

150ml/¼ pint/⅔ cup crème fraîche or
　　sour cream

salt and ground black pepper

45ml/3 tbsp chopped fresh chives,
　　to garnish

1 Put the cubed potatoes and chicken stock in a pan or flameproof casserole and bring to the boil over a medium heat. Reduce the heat and simmer for 15–20 minutes.

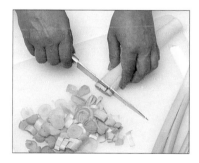

2 Make a slit along the length of each leek and rinse well under cold running water to wash away any soil. Slice thinly.

VARIATION
～

To make a low-fat soup, use low-fat fromage frais (farmer's cheese) instead of cream.

3 When the potatoes are barely tender, stir in the leeks. Taste, then season with salt and ground black pepper and simmer, stirring occasionally, for 10–15 minutes, until both the vegetables are soft. If the soup is too thick, thin it down with a little more chicken stock or water.

4 Process the soup in a blender or food processor. If you prefer a very smooth soup, pass it through a food mill or press through a coarse sieve. Stir in most of the cream and reheat gently, but do not boil. Ladle into warmed bowls and garnish with a swirl of cream and the chopped chives.

Spiced Mussel Soup

Chunky and colourful, this Turkish fish soup is like a chowder in its consistency. It is flavoured with harissa, which is more familiar in North African cookery.

INGREDIENTS

Serves 6

1.5kg/3–3½lb fresh mussels

150ml/¼ pint/⅔ cup white wine

30ml/2 tbsp olive oil

1 onion, finely chopped

2 garlic cloves, crushed

2 celery sticks, thinly sliced

bunch of spring onions (scallions), thinly sliced

1 potato, diced

7.5ml/1½ tsp harissa

3 tomatoes, peeled and diced

45ml/3 tbsp chopped fresh parsley

ground black pepper

thick natural (plain) yogurt, to serve

1 Scrub the mussels, discarding any damaged ones or any that do not close when tapped.

2 Bring the wine to the boil in a large, pan. Add the mussels and cover tightly with a lid. Cook, shaking the pan occasionally, for 4–5 minutes, until the mussel shells have opened wide. Discard any mussels that remain closed.

3 Drain the mussels, reserving the cooking liquid. Reserve a few mussels in their shells to use as a garnish and shell the rest.

4 Heat the oil in a pan and cook the onion, garlic, celery and spring onions for 5 minutes.

5 Add the shelled mussels, reserved liquid, potato, harissa and tomatoes. Bring to the boil, reduce the heat and cover. Simmer gently for 25 minutes.

6 Stir in the parsley and pepper and add the reserved mussels in their shells. Heat through for 1 minute. Serve immediately with a spoonful of yogurt.

Creamy Courgette and Dolcelatte Soup

The beauty of this soup is its delicate colour, its creamy texture and its subtle taste. If you prefer a more pronounced cheese flavour, use Gorgonzola instead of Dolcelatte.

INGREDIENTS

Serves 4–6

30ml/2 tbsp olive oil

15g/½oz/1 tbsp butter

1 onion, coarsely chopped

900g/2lb courgettes (zucchini), sliced

5ml/1 tsp dried oregano

about 600ml/1 pint/2½ cups
   Vegetable Stock

115g/4 oz Dolcelatte cheese, diced

300ml/½ pint/1¼ cups single
   (light) cream

salt and ground black pepper

To garnish

fresh oregano sprigs

extra Dolcelatte cheese

1 Heat the olive oil and butter in a large, heavy pan until foaming. Add the onion and cook over a medium heat for about 5 minutes, stirring frequently, until softened, but not brown.

2 Add the courgettes and oregano and season with salt and pepper to taste. Cook over a medium heat for 10 minutes, stirring frequently.

3 Pour in the stock and bring to the boil, stirring frequently. Lower the heat, half-cover the pan and simmer gently, stirring occasionally, for about 30 minutes. Stir in the diced Dolcelatte until it is melted.

4 Process the soup in a blender or food processor until smooth, then press through a sieve into a clean pan.

5 Add two-thirds of the cream and stir over a low heat until hot, but not boiling. Check the consistency and add more stock if the soup is too thick. Taste and adjust the seasoning if necessary.

6 Pour into heated bowls. Swirl in the remaining cream, garnish with fresh oregano and extra Dolcelatte cheese, crumbled, and serve immediately.

Fish Soup with Rouille

Making this soup is simplicity itself, yet the flavour suggests it is the product of painstaking preparation and complicated cooking.

Serves 6

1kg/2¼ lb mixed fish
30ml/2 tbsp olive oil
1 onion, chopped
1 carrot, chopped
1 leek, chopped
2 large ripe tomatoes, chopped
1 red (bell) pepper, seeded and chopped
2 garlic cloves, peeled
150g/5oz/⅔ cup tomato purée (paste)
1 large fresh bouquet garni, containing
    3 parsley sprigs, 3 small celery sticks
    and 3 bay leaves
300ml/½ pint/1¼ cups dry white wine
salt and ground black pepper

For the rouille

2 garlic cloves, coarsely chopped
5ml/1 tsp coarse salt
1 thick slice of white bread, crust
    removed, soaked in water and then
    squeezed dry
1 fresh red chilli, seeded and
    coarsely chopped
45ml/3 tbsp olive oil
pinch of cayenne pepper (optional)
salt

For the garnish

12 slices of baguette, toasted in the oven
50g/2oz/½ cup finely grated
    Gruyère cheese

COOK'S TIP

Any firm fish can be used for this recipe. If you use whole fish, include the heads, which enhance the flavour of the soup.

1 Cut the fish into 7.5cm/3in chunks, removing any obvious bones. Heat the olive oil in a large pan, then add the prepared fish and chopped vegetables. Stir gently until the vegetables are beginning to colour.

2 Now add all the other soup ingredients, then pour in just enough cold water to cover the mixture. Season well and bring to just below boiling point, then lower the heat so that the soup is barely simmering, cover and cook for 1 hour.

3 Meanwhile, make the rouille. Put the garlic and coarse salt in a mortar and crush to a paste with a pestle. Add the soaked bread and chilli and pound until smooth, or process in a food processor. Whisk in the olive oil, a drop at a time, to make a smooth, shiny sauce that resembles mayonnaise. Add a pinch of cayenne if you like and season to taste with salt. Set aside.

4 Lift out and discard the bouquet garni. Process the soup, in batches, in a food processor, then strain through a fine sieve into a clean pan, pushing the solids through with a ladle.

5 Reheat the soup, but do not boil. Taste and adjust the seasoning if necessary and ladle into individual bowls. Top each with two slices of toasted baguette, a spoonful of rouille and some grated Gruyère, then serve.

Tomato and Blue Cheese Soup

The concentrated flavour of roasted tomatoes strikes a great balance with strong blue cheese.

INGREDIENTS

Serves 4

1.5kg/3lb ripe tomatoes, peeled, quartered
    and seeded
2 garlic cloves, crushed
30ml/2 tbsp vegetable oil or butter
1 leek, chopped
1 carrot, chopped
1.2 litres/2 pints/5 cups Chicken Stock
115g/4 oz blue cheese, crumbled
45ml/3 tbsp whipping cream
several large fresh basil leaves or 1–2 fresh
    parsley sprigs, plus extra to garnish
salt and ground black pepper
175g/6 oz bacon, cooked and crumbled,
    to garnish

1 Preheat the oven to 200°C/400°F/Gas 6. Spread the tomatoes in a shallow ovenproof dish. Sprinkle with the garlic and some salt and pepper. Place in the oven and bake for 35 minutes.

2 Heat the oil or butter in a large pan. Add the leek and carrot and season lightly with salt and pepper. Cook over a low heat, stirring frequently, for about 10 minutes, until softened.

3 Stir in the stock and baked tomatoes. Bring to the boil, then lower the heat, cover and simmer for about 20 minutes.

4 Add the blue cheese, cream and basil or parsley. Transfer to a food processor or blender and process until smooth (work in batches if necessary). Taste and adjust the seasoning.

5 Reheat the soup, but do not boil. Serve garnished with bacon and a sprig of fresh herbs.

Fish Soup with Dumplings

Use a variety of whatever fish is available in this Czech soup, such as perch, catfish, cod or snapper. The basis of the dumplings is the same, whether you use semolina or flour.

INGREDIENTS

Serves 4–8

3 rindless bacon rashers (strips), diced

675g/1½ lb assorted fresh fish, skinned, boned and diced

15ml/1 tbsp paprika, plus extra to garnish

1.5 litres/2½ pints/6¼ cups Fish Stock or water

3 firm tomatoes, peeled and chopped

4 waxy potatoes, grated

5–10ml/1–2 tsp chopped fresh marjoram, plus extra to garnish

For the dumplings

75g/3oz/½ cup semolina or plain (all-purpose) flour

1 egg, beaten

45ml/3 tbsp milk or water

generous pinch of salt

15ml/1 tbsp chopped fresh parsley

1 Dry-fry the bacon in a large pan until golden brown, then add the pieces of assorted fish. Cook for 1–2 minutes, taking care not to break up the pieces of fish.

2 Sprinkle in the paprika, pour in the fish stock or water and bring to the boil. Reduce the heat and simmer for 10 minutes.

3 Stir the chopped tomatoes, grated potato and marjoram into the pan. Cook for 10 minutes, stirring occasionally.

4 Combine all the dumpling ingredients, then leave to stand, covered with clear film (plastic wrap) for 5–10 minutes.

5 Drop spoonfuls of the mixture into the soup and cook for 10 minutes. Serve hot with a little marjoram and paprika.

Cream of Mushroom Soup

A good mushroom soup makes the most of the subtle and sometimes rather elusive flavour of mushrooms. Button mushrooms are used here for their pale colour; chestnut or, better still, field mushrooms give a fuller flavour, but turn the soup brown.

INGREDIENTS

Serves 4

275g/10oz button (white) mushrooms
15ml/1 tbsp sunflower oil
40g/1½oz/3 tbsp butter
1 small onion, finely chopped
15ml/1 tbsp plain (all-purpose) flour
450ml/¾ pint/scant 2 cups Vegetable Stock
450ml/¾ pint/scant 2 cups milk
pinch of dried basil
30–45ml/2–3 tbsp single (light) cream
salt and ground black pepper
fresh basil leaves, to garnish

1 Separate the mushroom caps from the stalks. Finely slice the caps and finely chop the stalks.

2 Heat the oil and half the butter in a large, heavy pan and add the onion, mushroom stalks and about three-quarters of the sliced mushroom caps. Cook for about 1–2 minutes, stirring frequently, then cover and sweat over a gentle heat for 6–7 minutes, stirring occasionally.

3 Stir in the flour and cook for about 1 minute. Gradually add the stock and milk, stirring to make a smooth, thin sauce. Add the dried basil, and season to taste. Bring to the boil and simmer, partly covered, for 15 minutes.

4 Cool the soup slightly and then pour into a blender or food processor and process until smooth. Melt the remaining butter in a frying pan, add the remaining mushroom caps and cook gently for 3–4 minutes, until they are just tender.

5 Pour the soup into a clean pan and stir in the fried mushrooms. Heat until very hot. Taste and adjust the seasoning if necessary. Stir in the cream and heat briefly, but do not boil. Serve sprinkled with fresh basil leaves.

FISH &
SHELLFISH
SOUPS

Cream of Avocado Soup

*Avocados make wonderful soup –
pretty, delicious and refreshing.*

INGREDIENTS

Serves 4

2 large ripe avocados

1 litre/1¾ pints/4 cups Chicken Stock

250ml/8fl oz/1 cup single (light) cream

fresh coriander (cilantro) leaves

salt and freshly ground white pepper

1 Cut the avocados in half, remove the stones (pits) and scoop out the flesh. Mash the flesh, then put it into a sieve and press it through the sieve with a wooden spoon into a warm soup tureen.

2 Heat the chicken stock with the cream in a pan. When the mixture is hot, but not boiling, whisk it into the puréed avocado in the tureen.

3 Season to taste with salt and pepper. Serve immediately, sprinkled with the fresh coriander. The soup may be served chilled, if you like.

Eastern European Chickpea Soup

Chickpeas form part of the staple diet in the Balkans, where this soup originates. It is economical to make, and is a hearty and satisfying dish.

INGREDIENTS

Serves 4–6

500g/1¼lb/5 cups chickpeas, soaked overnight

2 litres/3½ pints/9 cups Vegetable Stock

3 large waxy potatoes, cut into bitesize chunks

50ml/2fl oz/¼ cup olive oil

225g/8oz spinach leaves

salt and ground black pepper

spicy sausage, cooked (optional)

1 Drain the chickpeas and rinse under cold water. Place in a large pan with the vegetable stock. Bring to the boil, then reduce the heat and cook gently for about 1 hour.

2 Add the potatoes and olive oil and season with salt and pepper to taste. Cook for about 20 minutes, until the potatoes are just tender.

3 Add the spinach and sliced, cooked sausage (if using) 5 minutes before the end of the cooking time. Ladle the soup into individual warmed soup bowls and serve immediately.

Carrot Soup with Ginger

The zing of fresh ginger is an ideal
complement to the sweetness of
cooked carrots.

INGREDIENTS

Serves 6

25g/1oz/2 tbsp butter or margarine
1 onion, chopped
1 celery stick, chopped
1 potato, chopped
675g/1½lb carrots, chopped
10ml/2 tsp crushed fresh root ginger
1.2 litres/2 pints/5 cups Chicken Stock
105ml/7 tbsp whipping cream
good pinch of freshly grated nutmeg
salt and ground black pepper

1 Put the butter or margarine,
onion and celery into a large
pan and cook for about 5 minutes,
until softened.

2 Stir in the potato, carrots,
ginger and stock. Bring to the
boil. Reduce the heat to low, cover
and simmer for about 20 minutes.

3 Pour the soup into a blender
or food processor and process
until it is smooth. Alternatively,
use a vegetable mill to purée the
soup. Return the soup to the pan.
Stir in the cream and nutmeg and
season with salt and pepper to
taste. Reheat gently, but do not
allow the soup to boil. Serve hot.

Chickpea and Spinach Soup with Garlic

This thick and creamy soup is richly flavoured – perfect for vegetarians.

Serves 4

30ml/2 tbsp olive oil

4 garlic cloves, crushed

1 onion, coarsely chopped

10ml/2 tsp ground cumin

10ml/2 tsp ground coriander

1.2 litres/2 pints/5 cups Vegetable Stock

350g/12oz potatoes, finely chopped

425g/15oz can chickpeas, drained

15ml/1 tbsp cornflour (cornstarch)

150ml/¼ pint/⅔ cup double (heavy) cream

30ml/2 tbsp light tahini

200g/7 oz spinach, shredded

cayenne pepper

salt and ground black pepper

2 Stir in the ground cumin and coriander and cook for 1 minute. Add the vegetable stock and potatoes. Bring to the boil and simmer for 10 minutes.

3 Add the chickpeas and simmer for a further 5 minutes, or until the potatoes are just tender.

4 Blend together the cornflour, cream, tahini and plenty of seasoning. Stir into the soup with the spinach. Bring to the boil, stirring, and simmer for a further 2 minutes. Adjust the seasoning with salt, pepper and cayenne to taste. Serve sprinkled with a little extra cayenne.

1 Heat the olive oil in a large, heavy pan and cook the garlic and onion over a medium heat, stirring occasionally, for about 5 minutes, or until the onion is softened and golden brown.

COOK'S TIP
~
Tahini is sesame seed paste and is available from many health food stores.

Red Pepper Soup with Lime

The beautiful, rich red colour of this soup makes it an attractive appetizer or light lunch. For a special dinner, toast some tiny croûtons and serve these sprinkled into the soup.

INGREDIENTS

Serves 4–6

1 large onion, chopped

4 red (bell) peppers, seeded and chopped

5 ml/1 tsp olive oil

1 garlic clove, crushed

1 small fresh red chilli, sliced

45 ml/3 tbsp tomato purée (paste)

900 ml/1½ pints/3¾ cups chicken stock

finely grated rind and juice of 1 lime

salt and freshly ground black pepper

shreds of lime rind, to garnish

1 Cook the onion and peppers gently in the oil in a covered pan for about 5 minutes, shaking the pan occasionally, until just softened.

2 Stir in the garlic, chilli and tomato purée. Add half the stock, then bring to the boil. Cover and simmer for 10 minutes.

3 Cool slightly, then purée in a food processor or blender. Return to the pan and add the remaining stock, the lime rind and juice and salt and pepper.

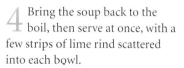

4 Bring the soup back to the boil, then serve at once, with a few strips of lime rind scattered into each bowl.

Chickpea and Parsley Soup

*Parsley and a hint of lemon bring
freshness to chickpeas.*

INGREDIENTS

Serves 6

225g/8oz/1⅓ cups chickpeas,
    soaked overnight
1 small onion
bunch of fresh parsley (about 40g/1½oz)
30ml/2 tbsp olive and sunflower
    oils, mixed
1.2 litres/2 pints/5 cups Chicken Stock
juice of ½ lemon
salt and ground black pepper
lemon wedges and finely pared strips of
    rind, to garnish

3 Heat the olive and sunflower
oils in a pan or flameproof
casserole and cook the onion
mixture over a low heat, stirring
frequently, for about 4 minutes
until the onion is slightly softened.

4 Add the chickpeas, cook gently
for 1–2 minutes, then add the
stock. Season with salt and pepper.
Bring the soup to the boil, then
cover and simmer for 20 minutes,
until the chickpeas are tender.

5 Leave the soup to cool a little
and then mash the chickpeas
with a fork until the soup is thick,
but still quite chunky.

6 Reheat the soup gently and
stir in the lemon juice. Serve
immediately, garnished with
lemon wedges and rind.

1 Drain the chickpeas and rinse
under cold water. Cook them
in boiling water for 1–1½ hours.
Drain and rub off the skins.

2 Place the onion and parsley in
a food processor or blender
and process until finely chopped.

Pear and Watercress Soup

The sweetness of the pears in the soup is complemented beautifully by Stilton croûtons. Their flavours make them natural partners.

INGREDIENTS

Serves 6

1 bunch of watercress
4 pears, peeled, cored
    and sliced
900ml/1½ pints/3¾ cups Chicken Stock
120ml/4fl oz/½ cup double (heavy) cream
juice of 1 lime
salt and ground black pepper

For the croûtons
25g/1oz/2 tbsp butter
15ml/1 tbsp olive oil
200g/7oz/3 cups cubed stale bread
150g/5oz/1 cup chopped Stilton cheese

1 Reserve about a third of the watercress leaves. Place the rest of the leaves and stalks in a pan with the pears, stock and a little seasoning. Simmer for about 15–20 minutes. Reserving some watercress leaves for garnishing, add the rest of the leaves and then process in a blender or food processor until smooth.

2 Put the mixture into a bowl and stir in the cream and the lime juice to mix the flavours thoroughly. Taste and adjust the seasoning if necessary. Pour all the soup back into a clean pan and reheat, stirring gently until warmed through.

3 To make the croûtons, melt the butter with the olive oil in a frying pan and cook the bread cubes until golden brown. Drain on kitchen paper. Put the cheese on top and heat under a hot grill (broiler) until bubbling. Reheat the soup and pour into bowls. Divide the croûtons and the reserved watercress leaves among the bowls and serve immediately.

Moroccan Harira

This tasty soup is traditionally eaten during the month of Ramadan, when the Muslim population fasts between sunrise and sunset.

INGREDIENTS

Serves 4

25g/1oz/2 tbsp butter
225g/8oz lamb, cut into 1cm/½in pieces
1 onion, chopped
450g/1lb well-flavoured tomatoes
60ml/4 tbsp chopped fresh
    coriander (cilantro)
30ml/2 tbsp chopped fresh parsley
2.5ml/½ tsp ground turmeric
2.5ml/½ tsp ground cinnamon
50g/2oz/¼ cup red lentils
75g/3 oz/½ cup chickpeas,
    soaked overnight
600ml/1 pint/2½ cups water
4 baby (pearl) onions, peeled
25g/1oz/¼ cup soup noodles
salt and ground black pepper

For the garnish
chopped fresh coriander (cilantro)
lemon slices
ground cinnamon

1 Heat the butter in a large pan or flameproof casserole and cook the lamb and chopped onion for 5 minutes, stirring frequently.

2 Peel the tomatoes, if you like, by plunging them into boiling water to loosen the skins. Wait for them to cool a little before peeling off the skins. Then cut them into quarters and add to the lamb with the herbs and spices.

3 Rinse the lentils under cold running water and drain the chickpeas. Add both to the pan with the water. Season with salt and pepper. Bring to the boil, cover and simmer gently for 1½ hours.

4 Add the baby onions and cook for a further 30 minutes. Add the noodles 5 minutes before the end of the cooking time. Serve the soup when the noodles are tender. Ladle into warm bowls, garnish with the coriander, lemon slices and cinnamon.

Bean, Lentil & Chickpea Soups

Spiced Parsnip Soup

This pale, creamy textured soup is given a special touch with an aromatic, spiced garlic and coriander garnish.

INGREDIENTS

Serves 4–6

40g/1½oz/3 tbsp butter
1 onion, chopped
675g/1½lb parsnips, diced
5ml/1 tsp ground coriander
2.5ml/½ tsp ground cumin
2.5ml/½ tsp ground turmeric
1.5ml/¼ tsp chilli powder
1.2 litres/2 pints/5 cups Chicken Stock
150ml/¼ pint/⅔ cup single (light) cream
15ml/1 tbsp sunflower oil
1 garlic clove, cut into julienne strips
10ml/2 tsp yellow mustard seeds
salt and ground black pepper

1 Melt the butter in a large pan, add the onion and parsnips and cook gently for 3 minutes.

2 Stir in the spices and cook for 1 minute more. Add the stock, season with salt and pepper to taste and bring to the boil.

3 Reduce the heat, cover and simmer for about 45 minutes, until the parsnips are tender. Cool slightly, then process the soup in a blender or food processor until smooth. Return the soup to the pan, add the cream and heat through gently over a low heat, but do not allow to boil.

4 Heat the oil in a small pan, add the julienne strips of garlic and the yellow mustard seeds and fry quickly until the garlic is beginning to brown and the mustard seeds start to pop and splutter. Remove from the heat.

5 Ladle the soup into warmed soup bowls and pour a little of the hot spice mixture over each one. Serve immediately.

Creamed Vegetable Soups

Chickpea and Pasta Soup

This is a simple, country-style soup, packed with flavour. The shape of the pasta and the beans complement one another beautifully.

INGREDIENTS

Serves 4–6

60ml/4 tbsp olive oil

1 onion, finely chopped

2 carrots, finely chopped

2 celery sticks, finely chopped

400g/14oz can chickpeas, drained
and rinsed

200g/7oz can cannellini beans, drained
and rinsed

150ml/¼ pint/⅔ cup passata (bottled
strained tomatoes)

120ml/4fl oz/½ cup water

1.5 litres/2½ pints/6¼ cups Vegetable or
Chicken Stock

1 fresh rosemary sprig, extra to garnish

200g/7oz/scant 2 cups dried conchiglie

salt and ground black pepper

shavings of Parmesan cheese, to serve

1 Heat the olive oil in a large, heavy pan, add the chopped vegetables and cook over a low heat, stirring frequently, for 5–7 minutes.

2 Add the chickpeas and cannellini beans, stir well to mix, then cook for 5 minutes. Stir in the passata and water. Cook, stirring, for 2–3 minutes.

3 Add 475ml/16fl oz/2 cups of the stock, the rosemary sprig and salt and ground black pepper to taste. Bring to the boil, cover, then simmer over a low heat, stirring occasionally, for 1 hour.

VARIATIONS

You can use other pasta shapes, but conchiglie are ideal because they scoop up the chickpeas and beans. If you like, crush 1–2 garlic cloves and cook them with the vegetables.

4 Pour in the remaining stock, add the pasta and bring to the boil. Lower the heat and simmer for 7–8 minutes, or according to the instructions on the packet, until the pasta is *al dente*. Remove the rosemary sprig. Serve the soup sprinkled with rosemary leaves and Parmesan shavings.

Mushroom and Bread Soup with Parsley

Thickened with bread, this rich mushroom soup will warm you up on cold winter days.

INGREDIENTS

Serves 8

75g/3 oz/6 tbsp unsalted (sweet) butter

900g/2lb field (portabello) mushrooms, sliced

2 onions, coarsely chopped

600ml/1 pint/2½ cups milk

8 slices white bread

60ml/4 tbsp chopped fresh parsley

300ml/½ pint/1¼ cups double (heavy) cream

salt and ground black pepper

1 Melt the butter in a large pan, add the sliced mushrooms and chopped onions and cook over a low heat, stirring occasionally, for about 10 minutes, until soft but not browned. Add the milk.

2 Tear the bread into pieces, drop them into the soup and leave to soak for 15 minutes. Purée the soup and return it to the pan. Add 45ml/3 tbsp of the parsley, the cream and seasoning. Reheat, without boiling. Serve garnished with the remaining parsley.

Smoked Turkey and Lentil Soup

Lentils seem to enhance the flavour of smoked turkey, and combined with four tasty vegetables they make a fine appetizer.

INGREDIENTS

Serves 4

25g/1oz/2 tbsp butter

1 large carrot, chopped

1 onion, chopped

1 leek, white part only, chopped

1 celery stick, chopped

115g/4oz/1½ cups mushrooms, chopped

50ml/2fl oz/¼ cup dry white wine

1.2 litres/2 pints/5 cups Chicken Stock

10ml/2 tsp dried thyme

1 bay leaf

115g/4oz/½ cup green lentils, rinsed

75g/3oz smoked turkey meat, diced

salt and ground black pepper

1 Melt the butter in a large pan. Add the carrot, onion, leek, celery and mushrooms. Cook over a medium heat, stirring frequently, for 3–5 minutes, until softened and golden brown.

2 Stir in the wine and chicken stock. Bring to the boil and skim off any foam that rises to the surface. Add the thyme and bay leaf. Lower the heat, cover and simmer gently for 30 minutes.

3 Add the lentils, re-cover the pan and continue cooking over a low heat for 30–40 minutes more, until they are just tender. Stir the soup occasionally to prevent the lentils from sticking to the base of the pan.

4 Stir in the smoked turkey and season to taste with salt and pepper. Cook until just heated through. Ladle the soup into bowls and serve immediately.

Baby Carrot and Fennel Soup

Sweet tender carrots find their moment of glory in this delicately spiced soup. Fennel provides a very subtle aniseed flavour that does not overpower the carrots.

INGREDIENTS

Serves 4

50g/2oz/4 tbsp butter

1 small bunch of spring onions (scallions), chopped

150g/5oz fennel bulb, chopped

1 celery stick, chopped

450g/1lb baby carrots, grated

2.5ml/½ tsp ground cumin

150g/5oz new potatoes, diced

1.2 litres/2 pints/5 cups Chicken Stock

60ml/4 tbsp double (heavy) cream

salt and ground black pepper

60ml/4 tbsp chopped fresh parsley, to garnish

1 Melt the butter in a large pan and add the spring onions, fennel, celery, carrots and cumin. Cover and cook over a low heat, stirring occasionally, for about 5 minutes, or until soft.

COOK'S TIP

For convenience, you can freeze the soup in portions before adding the cream, seasoning and parsley.

2 Add the diced potatoes and chicken stock, and gently simmer the mixture for a further 10 minutes.

3 Purée the soup in the pan with a hand-held blender. Stir in the cream and season to taste. Serve in individual soup bowls and garnish with chopped parsley.

Lentil Soup with Rosemary

A classic rustic Italian soup flavoured with rosemary, this is delicious served with garlic bread.

INGREDIENTS

Serves 4

225g/8oz/1 cup dried green or
    brown lentils
45ml/3 tbsp extra virgin olive oil
3 rindless streaky (fatty) bacon rashers
    (strips), cut into small dice
1 onion, finely chopped
2 celery sticks, finely chopped
2 carrots, finely chopped
2 fresh rosemary sprigs, finely chopped
2 bay leaves
400g/14oz can plum tomatoes
1.75 litres/3 pints/7½ cups
    Vegetable Stock
salt and ground black pepper
fresh bay leaves and fresh rosemary
    sprigs, to garnish

1 Place the lentils in a bowl and cover with cold water. Leave to soak for 2 hours. Rinse and drain.

2 Heat the olive oil in a large, heavy pan. Add the bacon and cook over a medium heat, stirring occasionally, for about 3 minutes, then add the onion and cook, stirring frequently, for 5 minutes, until softened.

3 Stir in the chopped celery, carrots, herbs and lentils. Toss over the heat for 1 minute, until thoroughly coated in the oil.

4 Tip in the tomatoes and stock, and bring to the boil. Lower the heat, half-cover the pan and simmer for about 1 hour, until the lentils are perfectly tender.

5 Remove and discard the bay leaves and season the soup with salt and pepper to taste. Ladle into warm bowls and serve hot with a garnish of fresh bay leaves and sprigs of rosemary.

COOK'S TIP

Keep an eye open for the small, flat green lentils in Italian groceries or delicatessens, as they have an excellent flavour.

Squash Soup with Horseradish Cream

The combination of cream, curry powder and horseradish makes a wonderful topping for this beautiful golden soup.

INGREDIENTS

Serves 6

1 butternut squash

1 cooking apple

25g/1oz/2 tbsp butter

1 onion, finely chopped

5–10ml/1–2 tsp curry powder, plus extra
    to garnish

900ml/1½ pints/3¾ cups Vegetable Stock

5ml/1 tsp chopped fresh sage

150ml/¼ pint/⅔ cup apple juice

salt and ground black pepper

lime shreds, to garnish (optional)

For the horseradish cream

60ml/4 tbsp double (heavy) cream

10ml/2 tsp horseradish sauce

2.5ml/½ tsp curry powder

1 Peel the squash, remove the seeds and chop the flesh. Peel, core and chop the apple.

2 Melt the butter in a large pan. Add the onion and cook over a medium heat, stirring frequently, for 5 minutes, until soft. Stir in the curry powder. Cook to bring out the flavour, stirring constantly, for 2 minutes.

3 Add the stock, squash, apple and sage. Bring to the boil, lower the heat, cover and simmer for 20 minutes, until the squash and apple are soft.

4 Meanwhile, make the horse-radish cream. Whip the cream in a bowl until stiff, then stir in the horseradish sauce and curry powder. Cover and chill until required.

5 Process the soup in a blender or food processor. Return to the clean pan and add the apple juice, with salt and pepper to taste. Reheat gently, without boiling.

6 Serve the soup in warm bowls, topped with a spoonful of horseradish cream and a dusting of curry powder. Garnish with a few lime shreds, if you like.

Garlicky Lentil Soup

High in fibre and protein, lentils make a particularly tasty soup and this recipe just couldn't be simpler or easier.

INGREDIENTS

Serves 6

225g/8 oz/1 cup red lentils, rinsed
   and drained
2 onions, finely chopped
2 large garlic cloves, finely chopped
1 carrot, finely chopped
30ml/2 tbsp olive oil
2 bay leaves
generous pinch of dried marjoram
   or oregano
1.5 litres/2½ pints/6¼ cups
   Vegetable Stock
30ml/2 tbsp red wine vinegar
salt and ground black pepper
celery leaves, to garnish
crusty bread rolls, to serve

1 Put all the ingredients except for the red wine vinegar, seasoning and garnish in a large, heavy pan. Bring to the boil over a medium heat, then lower the heat and simmer for 1½ hours, stirring the soup occasionally to prevent the lentils from sticking to the base of the pan.

2 Remove the bay leaves and add the red wine vinegar, with salt and pepper to taste. If the soup is too thick, thin it with a little extra vegetable stock or water. Ladle the soup into heated bowls and garnish with celery leaves. Serve immediately with warmed crusty rolls.

COOK'S TIP

If you buy your lentils loose, remember to tip them into a sieve or colander and pick them over, removing any pieces of grit, before rinsing them.

Jerusalem Artichoke Soup

Topped with saffron cream, this soup is wonderful on a chilly day.

INGREDIENTS

Serves 4

50g/2oz/4 tbsp butter

1 onion, chopped

450g/1lb Jerusalem artichokes, peeled and cut into chunks

900ml/1½ pints/3¾ cups Chicken Stock

150ml/¼ pint/⅔ cup milk

150ml/¼ pint/⅔ cup double (heavy) cream

good pinch of saffron powder

salt and ground black pepper

chopped fresh chives, to garnish

1 Melt the butter in a large, heavy pan and cook the onion for 5–8 minutes, until soft but not browned, stirring occasionally.

2 Add the Jerusalem artichokes to the pan and stir until coated in the butter. Cover and cook gently for 10–15 minutes, but do not allow the artichokes to brown.

3 Pour in the chicken stock and milk, then cover and simmer for 15 minutes. Cool slightly, then process in a blender or food processor until smooth.

4 Strain the soup back into the pan. Add half the cream, season to taste with salt and pepper and reheat gently. Lightly whip the remaining cream and the saffron powder. Ladle the soup into warmed soup bowls and put a spoonful of saffron cream in the centre of each. Sprinkle the chopped chives over the top and serve immediately.

Lentil and Bacon Soup

This is a wonderfully hearty German soup, but a lighter version can be made by omitting the frankfurters, if you like.

INGREDIENTS

Serves 6

225g/8oz/1 cup brown lentils

15ml/1 tbsp sunflower oil

1 onion, finely chopped

1 leek, finely chopped

1 carrot, finely diced

2 celery sticks, chopped

115g/4oz piece lean bacon

2 bay leaves

1.5 litres/2½ pints/6¼ cups water

30ml/2 tbsp chopped fresh parsley, plus extra to garnish

225g/8oz frankfurters, sliced

salt and ground black pepper

1 Rinse the lentils thoroughly under cold running water, then drain.

2 Heat the oil in a large pan and gently cook the onion , stirring occasionally, for 5 minutes, until soft. Add the leek, carrot, celery, bacon and bay leaves.

COOK'S TIP

Unlike most pulses, brown lentils do not need to be soaked before cooking.

3 Add the lentils. Pour in the water, then gradually bring to the boil. Skim the surface, then simmer, half-covered, for about 45–50 minutes, or until the lentils are soft.

4 Remove the piece of bacon from the soup and cut into small cubes. Trim off any fat.

5 Return the bacon to the soup with the parsley and sliced frankfurters, and season well with salt and ground black pepper. Simmer for 2–3 minutes, then remove the bay leaves.

6 Transfer to individual soup bowls and serve garnished with chopped parsley.

Watercress Soup

A delicious and nutritious soup which should be served with crusty bread.

Serves 4

15ml/1 tbsp sunflower oil

15g/¹/₂oz/1 tbsp butter

1 onion, finely chopped

1 potato, diced

about 175g/6oz watercress

400ml/14fl oz/1²/₃ cups Vegetable Stock

400ml/14fl oz/1²/₃ cups milk

lemon juice, to taste

salt and ground black pepper

sour cream, to serve

1 Heat the oil and butter in a large, heavy pan and cook the onion over a gentle heat for about 5 minutes, until soft, but not browned. Add the potato, cook gently for 2–3 minutes and then cover and sweat for 5 minutes over a gentle heat, stirring occasionally.

2 Strip the watercress leaves from the stalks and coarsely chop the stalks.

COOK'S TIP

Provided you leave out the sour cream, this is a low-calorie soup.

---

3 Add the stock and milk to the pan, stir in the chopped watercress stalks and season to taste with salt and pepper. Bring to the boil, lower the heat and simmer gently, partially covered, for 10–12 minutes, until the potatoes are tender. Add all but a few of the watercress leaves and simmer for 2 minutes more.

4 Process the soup in a blender or food processor, then pour into a clean pan and heat gently with the reserved watercress leaves.

5 Taste the soup when hot, add a little lemon juice and adjust the seasoning.

6 Pour the soup into warmed soup bowls and garnish with a little sour cream in the centre just before serving.

Lentil and Pasta Soup

Serve this rustic, vegetarian soup before a salad or other light main course. It goes well with Granary or crusty Italian bread.

INGREDIENTS

Serves 4–6

175g/6oz/³⁄₄ cup brown lentils

3 garlic cloves

1 litre/1³⁄₄ pints/4 cups water

45ml/3 tbsp olive oil

25g/1oz/2 tbsp butter

1 onion, finely chopped

2 celery sticks, finely chopped

30ml/2 tbsp sun-dried tomato paste

1.75 litres/3 pints/7¹⁄₂ cups
   Vegetable Stock

few fresh marjoram leaves, plus extra
   to garnish

few fresh basil leaves

leaves from fresh thyme sprig

50g/2oz/¹⁄₂ cup small dried pasta shapes

salt and ground black pepper

1 Put the lentils in a large pan. Smash one of the garlic cloves (there's no need to peel it first) and add it to the lentils. Pour in the water and bring to the boil. Lower the heat to a gentle simmer and cook for about 20 minutes, stirring occasionally, until the lentils are just tender.

2 Tip the lentils into a sieve, remove the cooked garlic clove and set it aside.

3 Rinse the lentils under cold running water, then leave them to drain. Heat 30ml/2 tbsp of the olive oil with half of the butter in a large pan. Add the onion and celery and cook over a low heat, stirring frequently, for 5–7 minutes, until softened.

COOK'S TIP

Use green lentils instead of brown, if you like, but the orange or red ones are not so good for this soup because they tend to go mushy.

---

4 Crush the remaining garlic and peel and mash the reserved cooked garlic clove. Add them to the vegetables with the remaining oil, the sun-dried tomato paste and lentils. Stir, then add the stock, herbs and salt and pepper to taste. Bring to the boil, stirring. Simmer for 30 minutes, stirring occasionally.

5 Add the pasta and bring to the boil, stirring. Simmer, stirring frequently, for 7–8 minutes, or according to the instructions on the packet, until the pasta is *al dente*. Add the remaining butter and adjust the seasoning. Serve hot in warmed bowls, garnished with marjoram leaves.

SMOOTH
VEGETABLE
SOUPS

Indian Spiced Lentil Soup

A subtle blend of spices takes this warming soup to new heights. Serve it with crusty bread for a filling start to a winter supper.

INGREDIENTS

Serves 6

2 onions, finely chopped

2 garlic cloves, crushed

4 tomatoes, coarsely chopped

2.5ml/½ tsp ground turmeric

5ml/1 tsp ground cumin

6 cardamom pods

½ cinnamon stick

225g/8oz/1 cup red lentils, rinsed and drained

900ml/1½ pints/3¾ cups water

400g/14oz can coconut milk

15ml/1 tbsp lime juice

salt and ground black pepper

cumin seeds, to garnish

1 Put the onions, garlic, tomatoes, turmeric, cumin, cardamom pods, cinnamon, lentils and water into a pan. Bring to the boil, lower the heat, cover and simmer gently for 20 minutes, or until the lentils are soft.

2 Remove the cardamom pods and cinnamon stick, then process the mixture in a blender or food processor. Press the soup through a sieve, then return it to the clean pan.

3 Reserve a little of the coconut milk for the garnish and add the remainder to the pan with the lime juice. Stir well and season with salt and pepper. Reheat the soup without boiling. Swirl in the reserved coconut milk, garnish with cumin seeds and serve.

Fresh Mushroom Soup with Tarragon

*This is a light mushroom soup,
subtly flavoured with tarragon.*

INGREDIENTS

Serves 6

15g/¹/₂oz/1 tbsp butter or margarine

4 shallots, finely chopped

450g/1lb/6 cups chestnut mushrooms,
    finely chopped

300ml/¹/₂ pint/1¹/₄ cups Vegetable Stock

300ml/¹/₂ pint/ 1¹/₄ cups semi-skimmed
    (low-fat) milk

15–30ml/1–2 tbsp chopped fresh tarragon

30ml/2 tbsp dry sherry (optional)

salt and ground black pepper

fresh tarragon sprigs, to garnish

1 Melt the butter or margarine
in a large pan, add the shallots
and cook over a low heat, stirring
occasionally, for 5 minutes. Add
the mushrooms and cook gently
for 3 minutes, stirring. Add the
stock and milk.

2 Bring to the boil, then cover
and simmer gently for about
20 minutes, until the vegetables
are soft. Stir in the chopped
tarragon and season to taste with
salt and pepper.

3 Leave the soup to cool slightly,
then process in a blender or
food processor, in batches if
necessary, until smooth. Return
the soup to the rinsed pan and
reheat gently.

4 Stir in the sherry, if using,
then ladle into soup bowls and
serve garnished with tarragon.

VARIATION

If you like, use a mixture of
wild and button (white)
mushrooms instead.

Black and White Bean Soup

Although this soup takes a while to prepare, the results are so stunning that it is well worth the effort.

INGREDIENTS

Serves 8

350g/12oz/2 cups dried black beans,
   soaked overnight and drained
2.4 litres/4¼ pints/10½ cups water
6 garlic cloves, crushed
350g/12oz/2 cups dried white beans,
   soaked overnight and drained
90ml/6 tbsp balsamic vinegar
4 jalapeño peppers, seeded and chopped
6 spring onions (scallions), finely chopped
juice of 1 lime
50ml/2fl oz/¼ cup olive oil
15g/½oz/¼ cup chopped fresh coriander
   (cilantro), plus extra to garnish
salt and ground black pepper

1 Place the black beans in a large pan with half the water and garlic. Bring to the boil. Reduce the heat to low, cover the pan, and simmer for about 1½ hours, until the beans are soft.

2 Meanwhile, put the white beans in another pan with the remaining water and garlic. Bring to the boil, cover the pan and simmer for about 1 hour until soft.

3 Process the cooked white beans in a food processor or blender. Stir in the balsamic vinegar, jalapeños, and half the spring onions. Return to the pan and reheat gently.

4 Process the cooked black beans in the food processor or blender. Return to the pan and stir in the lime juice, olive oil, coriander and remaining spring onions. Reheat gently.

5 Season both soups with salt and ground black pepper to taste. To serve, place a ladleful of each puréed soup, side by side, in each of eight warmed soup bowls. Swirl the two soups together with a cocktail stick (toothpick) or skewer. Garnish with chopped fresh coriander and serve.

Broccoli and Almond Soup

The creaminess of the toasted almonds combines perfectly with the slightly bitter taste of the broccoli.

INGREDIENTS

Serves 4–6

50g/2oz/¹/₂ cup ground almonds

675g/1¹/₂lb broccoli

900ml/1¹/₂ pints/3³/₄ cups Vegetable Stock
    or water

300ml/¹/₂ pint/1¹/₄ cups skimmed milk

salt and ground black pepper

1 Preheat the oven to 180°C/ 350°F/ Gas 4. Spread the ground almonds evenly on a baking sheet and toast in the oven for about 10 minutes, until golden. Reserve one quarter of the toasted almonds and set aside to garnish the finished dish.

2 Cut the broccoli into small florets and steam for about 6–7 minutes, until tender.

3 Place the remaining toasted almonds, broccoli, vegetable stock or water and milk in a blender or food processor and process until smooth. Season with salt and pepper to taste.

4 Pour the soup into a pan and heat gently. Ladle into warm bowls and serve sprinkled with the reserved toasted almonds.

Bean and Pasta Soup

Serve this hearty soup with tasty, pesto-topped French bread croûtons.

INGREDIENTS

Serves 4

115g/4oz/½ cup mixed dried beans,
   soaked overnight and drained
15ml/1 tbsp oil
1 onion, chopped
2 celery sticks, thinly sliced
2–3 garlic cloves, crushed
2 leeks, thinly sliced
1 vegetable stock (bouillon) cube
400g/14oz can or jar pimientos
45–60ml/3–4 tbsp tomato purée (paste)
115g/4oz dried pasta shapes
4 slices French bread
15ml/1 tbsp pesto
115g/4oz/l cup baby corn cobs, halved
50g/2oz broccoli florets
50g/2oz cauliflower florets
a few drops of Tabasco sauce
salt and ground black pepper

3 Meanwhile, purée the pimientos with a little of their liquid and add to the pan. Stir in the tomato purée and pasta and cook for 15 minutes. Preheat the oven to 200°C/400°F/Gas 6.

4 Meanwhile, make the pesto croûtons. Spread the French bread with the pesto and bake for 10 minutes, or until crisp.

5 When the pasta is just cooked, add the corn cobs, broccoli, cauliflower, Tabasco and seasoning to taste. Heat for 2–3 minutes and serve with the pesto croûtons.

1 Place the beans in a large pan and cover with water. Bring to the boil and boil rapidly for 15 minutes. Drain and cover with fresh water. Bring to the boil, then simmer for about 45 minutes, or until nearly tender.

2 When the beans are almost ready, heat the oil in a large pan and cook the vegetables for 2 minutes. Add the stock cube and the beans with about 600ml/1 pint/ 2½ cups of their liquid. Cover and simmer for 10 minutes.

Fresh Tomato Soup

Intensely flavoured sun-ripened tomatoes need little embellishment in this fresh-tasting soup. If you buy from the supermarket, choose the juiciest looking ones and add the amount of sugar and vinegar necessary, depending on their natural sweetness. On a hot day, this Italian soup is also delicious chilled.

Serves 6

1.3–1.6kg/3–3½lb ripe tomatoes

400ml/14fl oz/1⅔ cups Chicken or
   Vegetable Stock

45ml/3 tbsp sun-dried tomato paste

30–45ml/2–3 tbsp balsamic vinegar

10–15ml/2–3 tsp caster (superfine) sugar

small handful of basil leaves

salt and ground black pepper

basil leaves, to garnish

toasted cheese croûtes and crème fraîche,
   to serve

1 Plunge the tomatoes into boiling water for 30 seconds, then refresh in cold water. Peel off the skins and quarter the tomatoes.

2 Put the tomatoes in a large pan and pour over the chicken or vegetable stock. Bring just to the boil, reduce the heat, cover and simmer the mixture gently for about 10 minutes, until the tomatoes are pulpy.

3 Stir in the sun-dried tomato paste, vinegar, sugar and basil. Season with salt and pepper, then cook gently, stirring, for 2 minutes. Process the soup in a blender or food processor, then return to the pan and reheat gently. Serve in warm bowls topped with one or two toasted cheese croûtes and a spoonful of crème fraîche and garnished with basil leaves.

Broad Bean and Rice Soup

This thick soup makes the most of fresh broad beans while they are in season. It works well with frozen beans for the rest of the year.

INGREDIENTS

Serves 4

1kg/2¼lb broad (fava) beans in their
    pods, or 400g/14 oz shelled frozen
    broad (fava) beans, thawed

90ml/6 tbsp olive oil

1 onion, finely chopped

2 tomatoes, peeled and
    finely chopped

225g/8 oz/1 cup arborio or other
    non-parboiled rice

25g/1oz/2 tbsp butter

1 litre/1¾ pints/4 cups boiling water

salt and ground black pepper

grated Parmesan cheese, to
    serve (optional)

1 Shell the beans if they are fresh. Bring a large pan of water to the boil and blanch the beans, fresh or frozen, for 3–4 minutes. Rinse under cold water and peel off the skins.

2 Heat the oil in a large pan. Add the onion and cook over a low to moderate heat until it softens. Stir in the beans and cook for about 5 minutes, stirring to coat them with the oil.

3 Season to taste with salt and pepper. Add the tomatoes and cook for a further 5 minutes, stirring frequently. Add the rice and cook, stirring constantly, for a further 1–2 minutes.

4 Add the butter and stir until it melts. Pour in the water, a little at a time. Adjust the seasoning to taste. Continue cooking until the rice is tender. Serve with grated Parmesan, if you like.

Nettle Soup

A country-style soup which is a tasty variation of the classic Irish potato soup. Use wild nettles if you can find them, or a washed head of round lettuce if you prefer.

INGREDIENTS

Serves 4

115g/4oz/¹/₂ cup butter
450g/1lb onions, sliced
450g/1lb potatoes, cut into chunks
750ml/1¹/₄ pints/3 cups Chicken Stock
25g/1oz/1 cup nettle leaves
small bunch of fresh chives, chopped
salt and ground black pepper
double (heavy) cream, to serve

2 Wearing rubber (latex) gloves, remove the nettle leaves from their stalks. Wash the leaves under cold running water, then dry on kitchen paper. Add to the pan and cook for a further 5 minutes.

3 Ladle the soup into a blender or food processor and process until smooth. Return to a clean pan and season well. Stir in the chives and serve with a swirl of cream and a sprinkling of pepper.

1 Melt the butter in a large pan and add the sliced onions. Cover and cook over a low heat for about 5 minutes, until softened. Add the potatoes to the pan with the chicken stock. Cover and cook for 25 minutes.

COOK'S TIP

If you like, cut the vegetables finely and leave the cooked soup chunky rather than puréeing it.

White Bean Soup

Use either haricot (navy) or butter (lima) beans for this velvety soup.

INGREDIENTS

Serves 4

175g/6oz/¾ cup dried white beans,
   soaked in cold water overnight
30–45ml/2–3 tbsp oil
2 large onions, chopped
4 celery sticks, chopped
1 parsnip, chopped
1 litre/1¾ pints/4 cups Chicken Stock
salt and ground black pepper
chopped fresh coriander (cilantro) and
   paprika, to garnish

1 Drain the beans and boil rapidly in fresh water for 10 minutes. Drain, cover with more fresh water and simmer for 1–2 hours, until soft. Reserve the liquid and discard any bean skins on the surface.

2 Heat the oil in a heavy pan and sauté the onions, celery and parsnip for 3 minutes.

3 Add the cooked beans and chicken stock to the pan and continue cooking until all the vegetables are tender. Remove the pan from the heat, leave the soup to cool slightly, then, using a food processor or hand blender, blend it until it is velvety smooth.

4 Reheat the soup gently, gradually adding some of the bean liquid or a little water if it is too thick. Season to taste.

5 To serve, transfer the soup into wide bowls. Garnish with fresh coriander and paprika.

COOK'S TIP

You can, if you like, use a 400g/14oz can cannellini or butter (lima) beans instead of dried beans. Drain and rinse them before adding to the dish.

Mushroom, Celery and Garlic Soup

A robust soup in which the dominant flavour of mushrooms is enhanced with garlic, while celery introduces a contrasting note.

INGREDIENTS

Serves 4

350g/12oz/4½ cups chopped mushrooms

4 celery sticks, chopped

3 garlic cloves

45ml/3 tbsp dry sherry or white wine

750ml/1¼ pints/3 cups Chicken Stock

30ml/2 tbsp Worcestershire sauce

5ml/1 tsp freshly grated nutmeg

salt and ground black pepper

celery leaves, to garnish

1 Place the mushrooms, celery and garlic in a pan and stir in the sherry or wine. Cover and cook over a low heat for 30–40 minutes, until the vegetables are tender.

2 Add half the stock and process in a food processor or blender until smooth. Return to the pan and add the remaining stock, the Worcestershire sauce and nutmeg.

3 Bring to the boil and season to taste with salt and pepper. Ladle the soup into warm bowls and serve immediately, garnished with celery leaves.

Beetroot and Butter Bean Soup

This soup is a simplified version of borscht and is prepared in a fraction of the time. Serve with a spoonful of sour cream and a sprinkling of chopped fresh parsley.

INGREDIENTS

Serves 4

30ml/2 tbsp vegetable oil

1 onion, sliced

5ml/l tsp caraway seeds

finely grated rind of ½ orange

250g/9oz cooked beetroot (beet), grated

1.2 litres/2 pints/5 cups Meat Stock
  or rassol (see Cook's Tip)

400g/14oz can butter (lima) beans,
  drained and rinsed

15ml/1 tbsp wine vinegar

60ml/4 tbsp sour cream

60ml/4 tbsp chopped fresh parsley,
  to garnish

1 Heat the oil in a large pan and cook the onion, caraway seeds and orange rind over a low heat until soft, but not coloured.

2 Add the beetroot, stock or rassol, butter beans and vinegar and simmer over a low heat for a further 10 minutes.

3 Divide the soup among four warm bowls, add a spoonful of sour cream to each, sprinkle with chopped parsley and serve.

COOK'S TIP

Rassol is a beetroot (beet) broth, which is used to impart a strong beetroot colour and flavour. You are most likely to find it in Kosher food stores.

Cauliflower and Walnut Soup

This classic combination works well in a number of dishes – especially this richly flavoured soup.

INGREDIENTS

Serves 4

1 cauliflower

1 onion, coarsely chopped

450ml/¾ pint/scant 2 cups Chicken or Vegetable Stock

450ml/¾ pint/scant 2 cups skimmed milk

45ml/3 tbsp walnut pieces

salt and ground black pepper

paprika and chopped walnuts, to garnish

1 Trim the cauliflower of outer leaves and break into small florets. Place the cauliflower, onion and stock in a large pan.

2 Bring to the boil, cover and simmer for about 15 minutes, until soft. Add the milk and walnut pieces, then process in a blender or food processor until smooth.

3 Season the soup to taste with salt and pepper, then reheat and bring to the boil. Serve hot sprinkled with a dusting of paprika and chopped walnuts.

VARIATION
❧

If you like, you can make this soup using broccoli instead of cauliflower.

Spicy Bean Soup

A filling soup made with two kinds of beans flavoured with cumin.

INGREDIENTS

Serves 6–8

175g/6oz/1 cup dried black beans, soaked overnight and drained
175g/6oz/1 cup dried kidney beans, soaked overnight and drained
2 bay leaves
90ml/6 tbsp coarse salt
30ml/2 tbsp olive or vegetable oil
3 carrots, chopped
1 onion, chopped
1 celery stick
1 garlic clove, crushed
5ml/1 tsp ground cumin
1.5–2.5ml/¼–½ tsp cayenne pepper
2.5ml/½ tsp dried oregano
50ml/2fl oz/¼ cup red wine
1.2 litres/2 pints/5 cups Meat Stock
250ml/8fl oz/1 cup water
salt and ground black pepper

For the garnish
sour cream
chopped fresh coriander (cilantro)

1 Put the black beans and kidney beans in two separate pans with cold water to cover and a bay leaf in each. Boil rapidly for 10 minutes, then cover and simmer for 20 minutes.

2 Add 45ml/3 tbsp coarse salt to each pan and continue simmering for 30 minutes, until the beans are tender. Drain.

3 Heat the oil in a large, heavy flameproof casserole. Add the carrots, onion, celery and garlic and cook over a low heat for 8–10 minutes, stirring, until softened. Stir in the cumin, cayenne, and oregano and season with salt to taste.

4 Add the red wine, meat stock and water and stir to mix all the ingredients together. Remove the bay leaves from the cooked beans and discard, then add the beans to the casserole.

5 Bring to the boil, reduce the heat, then cover and simmer gently for about 20 minutes, stirring occasionally.

6 Transfer half the soup (including most of the solids) to a food processor or blender. Process until smooth. Return to the pan and stir to combine well.

7 Reheat the soup and adjust the seasoning to taste. Serve hot, garnished with sour cream and chopped coriander.

Bean, Lentil & Chickpea Soups

Pumpkin Soup

The sweet flavour of pumpkin is excellent in soups, teaming well with other savoury ingredients, such as onions and potatoes, to make a warm and comforting dish. For added flavour, try roasting the pumpkin chunks instead before adding to the soup with the stock.

INGREDIENTS

Serves 4–6

15ml/1 tbsp sunflower oil

25g/1oz/2 tbsp butter

1 large onion, sliced

675g/1½lb pumpkin, cut into
  large chunks

450g/1 1b potatoes, sliced

600ml/1 pint/2½ cups Vegetable Stock

good pinch of freshly grated nutmeg

5ml/1 tsp chopped fresh tarragon

600ml/1 pint/2½ cups milk

5–10ml/1–2 tsp lemon juice

salt and ground black pepper

1 Heat the oil and butter in a heavy pan, add the onion and cook for 4–5 minutes over a gentle heat until soft but not browned, stirring frequently.

2 Add the pumpkin and sliced potatoes, stir well, then cover and sweat over a low heat for about 10 minutes, until the vegetables are almost tender, stirring occasionally to stop them sticking to the pan.

3 Stir in the vegetable stock, grated nutmeg and tarragon and season to taste with salt and pepper. Bring to the boil, then lower the heat and simmer for about 10 minutes, until the vegetables are completely tender.

4 Leave the soup to cool slightly, then pour into a blender or food processor and process until smooth. Pour back into a clean pan and add the milk. Heat gently and then taste, adding lemon juice to taste and extra seasoning, if necessary. Serve piping hot.

Chunky Bean and Vegetable Soup

A substantial soup, not unlike
minestrone, using a selection of
vegetables, with cannellini beans for
extra protein and fibre. Serve with a
hunk of wholegrain bread.

INGREDIENTS

Serves 4

30 ml/2 tbsp olive oil

2 celery sticks, chopped

2 leeks, sliced

3 carrots, sliced

2 garlic cloves, crushed

400 g/14 oz can chopped tomatoes with
    basil

1.2 litres/2 pints/5 cups vegetable stock

400 g/14 oz can cannellini beans (or
    mixed pulses), drained

15 ml/1 tbsp pesto sauce

salt and freshly ground black pepper

Parmesan cheese shavings, to serve

2 Stir in the tomatoes and stock.
Bring to the boil, then cover
and cook gently for 15 minutes.

3 Stir in the beans and pesto,
with salt and pepper to taste.
Heat through for a further
5 minutes. Serve in heated bowls,
sprinkled with shavings of
Parmesan cheese.

1 Heat the olive oil in a large
pan. Add the celery, leeks,
carrots and garlic and cook gently
for about 5 minutes until they
have softened.

COOK'S TIP

Extra vegetables can be added to
the soup to make it even more
substantial. For example, add
some thinly sliced courgettes
(zucchini) or finely shredded
cabbage for the last 5 minutes of
the cooking time. Or, stir in
some small wholewheat pasta
shapes. Add them at the same
time as the tomatoes, as they will
take 10–15 minutes to cook.

Moroccan Vegetable Soup

Creamy parsnip and pumpkin give this soup a wonderfully rich texture.

INGREDIENTS

Serves 4

15ml/1 tbsp olive or sunflower oil

15g/¹/₂oz/1 tbsp butter

1 onion, chopped

225g/8oz carrots, chopped

225g/8oz parsnips, chopped

225g/8oz pumpkin

about 900ml/1¹/₂ pints/3³/₄ cups Vegetable
    or Chicken Stock

lemon juice, to taste

salt and ground black pepper

For the garnish

7.5ml/1¹/₂ tsp olive oil

¹/₂ garlic clove, finely chopped

45ml/3 tbsp chopped fresh parsley and
    coriander (cilantro), mixed

good pinch of paprika

1 Heat the oil and butter in a large pan and cook the onion, stirring occasionally, for about 3 minutes, until softened. Add the carrots and parsnips, stir well, cover and cook over a gentle heat for a further 5 minutes.

2 Cut the pumpkin into chunks, discarding the skin and pith, and stir into the pan. Cover and cook for a further 5 minutes, then add the stock and seasoning and gradually bring to the boil. Cover and simmer for 35–40 minutes, until the vegetables are tender.

3 Leave the soup to cool slightly, then pour in to a blender or food processor and process until smooth, adding a little extra water or stock if the soup seems too thick. Pour back into a clean pan and reheat gently.

4 To make the garnish, heat the oil in a small pan and cook the garlic and herbs for 1–2 minutes. Add the paprika and stir well.

5 Taste and adjust the seasoning of the soup and stir in lemon juice to taste. Pour into bowls and spoon a little of the prepared garnish on top, which should then be swirled carefully into the soup.

Ribollita

Ribollita is rather like minestrone, but includes beans instead of pasta. In Italy, it is traditionally served ladled over bread and a rich green vegetable, although you could omit this for a lighter version.

INGREDIENTS

Serves 6–8

45ml/3 tbsp olive oil

2 onions, chopped

2 carrots, sliced

4 garlic cloves, crushed

2 celery sticks, thinly sliced

1 fennel bulb, trimmed and chopped

2 large courgettes (zucchini), thinly sliced

400g/14oz can chopped tomatoes

30ml/2 tbsp pesto, either home-made or
   ready-made

900ml/1½ pints/3¾ cups Vegetable Stock

400g/14oz can haricot (navy) or borlotti
   beans, drained

salt and ground black pepper

To serve

450g/1 lb young spinach

15ml/1 tbsp extra virgin olive oil, plus
   extra for drizzling

6–8 slices white bread

Parmesan cheese shavings (optional)

1 Heat the oil in a large, heavy pan. Add the onions, carrots, garlic, celery and fennel and cook over a low heat, stirring frequently, for 10 minutes. Add the courgette slices and cook, stirring, for a further 2 minutes.

2 Add the chopped tomatoes, pesto, vegetable stock and beans and bring to the boil. Reduce the heat, cover and simmer gently for 25–30 minutes, until all the vegetables are tender. Season with salt and ground black pepper to taste.

3 To serve, cook the spinach in the oil for 2 minutes, or until wilted. Spoon over the bread in soup bowls, then ladle the soup over the spinach. Serve with extra olive oil for drizzling on to the soup and Parmesan cheese to sprinkle on top, if you like.

Sweet Potato and Parsnip Soup

*The natural sweetness of these
two popular root vegetables comes
through very strongly in this
delicious soup.*

INGREDIENTS

Serves 6

15ml/1 tbsp sunflower oil
1 large leek, sliced
2 celery sticks, chopped
450g/1lb sweet potatoes, diced
225g/8oz parsnips, diced
900ml/1½ pints/3¾ cups Vegetable Stock
salt and ground black pepper

For the garnish
15ml/1 tbsp chopped fresh parsley
roasted strips of sweet potatoes
  and parsnips

1 Heat the oil in a large pan and
add the leek, celery, sweet
potatoes and parsnips. Cook gently
for about 5 minutes, stirring to
prevent them from browning or
sticking to the pan.

2 Stir in the vegetable stock and
bring to the boil, then cover
and simmer over a low heat for
about 25 minutes, or until the
vegetables are tender, stirring
occasionally. Season to taste with
salt and pepper . Remove the pan
from the heat and leave the soup to
cool slightly.

3 Process the soup in a blender
or food processor until
smooth, then return it to the pan
and reheat gently. Ladle into
warmed soup bowls to serve and
sprinkle over the chopped fresh
parsley and roasted strips of sweet
potatoes and parsnips.

Tuscan Bean Soup

There are many versions of this wonderful soup. This one uses cannellini beans, leeks, cabbage and good olive oil – and tastes even better when it is reheated.

INGREDIENTS

Serves 4

45ml/3 tbsp extra virgin olive oil

1 onion, coarsely chopped

2 leeks, coarsely chopped

1 large potato, diced

2 garlic cloves, finely chopped

1.2 litres/2 pints/5 cups Vegetable Stock

400g/14oz can cannellini beans, drained and can juice reserved

175g/6oz Savoy cabbage, shredded

45ml/3 tbsp chopped fresh flat leaf parsley

30ml/2 tbsp chopped fresh oregano

75g/3oz/1 cup shaved Parmesan cheese

salt and ground black pepper

For the garlic toasts

30–45ml/2–3 tbsp extra virgin olive oil

6 thick slices country bread

1 garlic clove, peeled and bruised

1 Heat the oil in a large, heavy pan, add the onion, leeks, potato and garlic and cook over a low heat, stirring occasionally, for 4–5 minutes, until they are just beginning to soften.

2 Pour on the vegetable stock and the reserved can juice from the beans. Cover and simmer for 15 minutes.

3 Stir in the cabbage, beans and half the herbs, season and cook for a further 10 minutes. Spoon about one-third of the soup into a food processor or blender and process until fairly smooth. Return to the soup in the pan, adjust the seasoning and heat through for 5 minutes.

4 Make the garlic toasts. Drizzle a little oil over the slices of bread, then rub both sides of each slice with the garlic. Toast until browned on both sides. Ladle the soup into bowls. Sprinkle with the remaining herbs and the Parmesan shavings. Add a drizzle of olive oil and serve with the hot garlic toasts.

Sweet Potato and Red Pepper Soup

As colourful as it is good to eat, this soup is a sure winner, whether for a midweek family supper or a dinner-party first course.

INGREDIENTS

Serves 6

2 red (bell) peppers (about 225g/8 oz) seeded and cubed

500g/1¼lb sweet potatoes, cubed

1 onion, coarsely chopped

2 large garlic cloves, coarsely chopped

300ml/½ pint/1¼ cups dry white wine

1.2 litres/2 pints/5 cups Vegetable Stock

Tabasco sauce, to taste

salt and ground black pepper

fresh country bread, to serve

1 Dice a small quantity of red pepper for the garnish and set aside. Put the rest into a pan with the sweet potato, onion, garlic, wine and vegetable stock. Bring to the boil, lower the heat and simmer for 30 minutes, or until all the vegetables are quite soft. Leave to cool slightly.

2 Transfer the mixture to a blender or food processor and process until smooth. Season to taste with salt, pepper and a generous dash of Tabasco.

3 Leave to cool to serve warm or at room temperature. Garnish with the reserved diced red pepper.

Beef Chilli Soup

This is a hearty dish based on a traditional chilli recipe. It is ideal served with fresh, crusty bread as a warming start to any meal.

Serves 4

15ml/1 tbsp oil

1 onion, chopped

175g/6oz/¾ cup minced (ground) beef

2 garlic cloves, chopped

1 fresh red chilli, sliced

25g/1oz/¼ cup plain (all-purpose) flour

400g/14oz can chopped tomatoes

600ml/1 pint/2½ cups Meat Stock

225g/8oz/2 cups canned kidney beans, drained and rinsed

30ml/2 tbsp chopped fresh parsley

salt and ground black pepper

crusty bread, to serve

1 Heat the oil in a large pan. Add the onion and minced beef and cook for 5 minutes, until brown and sealed.

2 Add the garlic, chilli and flour. Cook for 1 minute. Add the tomatoes and pour in the stock. Bring to the boil.

COOK'S TIP
~

For a milder flavour, remove the seeds from the chilli after slicing.

3 Stir in the kidney beans and season with salt and pepper to taste. Lower the heat and simmer for 20 minutes.

4 Add the chopped parsley, reserving a little to garnish the finished dish. Pour the soup into warm bowls, sprinkle with the reserved parsley and serve with crusty bread.

Cauliflower, Flageolet and Fennel Seed Soup

The sweet, anise-liquorice flavour of the fennel seeds gives a delicious edge to this hearty soup.

INGREDIENTS

Serves 4–6

15ml/1 tbsp olive oil

1 garlic clove, crushed

1 onion, chopped

10ml/2 tsp fennel seeds

1 cauliflower, cut into small florets

2 x 400g/14 oz cans flageolet or cannellini beans, drained and rinsed

1.2 litres/2 pints/5 cups Vegetable Stock or water

salt and ground black pepper

chopped fresh parsley, to garnish

toasted slices of French bread, to serve

3 Bring the mixture to the boil. Reduce the heat and simmer for about 10 minutes, or until the cauliflower is tender. Leave to cool slightly, then pour the soup into a blender or food processor and process until smooth.

4 Stir in the remaining beans and season to taste with salt and pepper. Reheat the soup and pour into warmed bowls. Sprinkle with chopped parsley and serve immediately with toasted slices of French bread.

1 Heat the olive oil. Add the garlic, onion and fennel seeds and cook gently for 5 minutes, or until the onion is softened.

2 Add the cauliflower florets, half the beans and the vegetable stock or water.

Lamb, Bean and Pumpkin Soup

This is a hearty soup to warm the cockles of the heart.

INGREDIENTS

Serves 4

115g/4oz/²⁄₃ cup split black-eyed beans
   (peas), soaked overnight
675g/1¹⁄₂lb neck (US shoulder or breast)
   of lamb, cut into medium-sized chunks
5ml/1 tsp chopped fresh thyme or
   2.5ml/¹⁄₂ tsp dried thyme
2 bay leaves
1.2 litres/2 pints/5 cups Meat Stock
1 onion, sliced
225g/8oz pumpkin, diced
2 black cardamom pods
7.5ml/1¹⁄₂ tsp ground turmeric
15ml/1 tbsp chopped fresh
   coriander (cilantro)
2.5ml/¹⁄₂ tsp caraway seeds
1 fresh green chilli, seeded and chopped
2 green bananas
1 carrot
salt and ground black pepper

1 Drain the black-eyed beans, place them in a pan and cover with fresh cold water.

2 Bring the beans to the boil, boil rapidly for 10 minutes and then reduce the heat and simmer, covered, for about 40–50 minutes, until tender, adding more water if necessary. Remove the pan from the heat and set aside to cool.

3 Meanwhile, put the lamb in a large pan, add the thyme, bay leaves and stock and bring to the boil. Cover and simmer over a moderate heat for 1 hour, until the meat is tender.

4 Add the onion, pumpkin, cardamoms, turmeric, coriander, caraway, chilli and seasoning and stir. Bring back to a simmer and cook, uncovered, for 15 minutes, stirring occasionally, until the pumpkin is tender.

5 When the beans are cool, spoon into a blender or food processor with their liquid and process to a smooth purée.

6 Peel the bananas and cut into medium slices. Cut the carrot into thin slices. Stir the banana and carrot slices into the soup with the beans and cook for 10–12 minutes, until the carrot is tender. Adjust the seasoning if necessary, ladle into a warm tureen or individual bowls and serve immediately.

Root Vegetable Soup

Simmer a selection of popular and inexpensive winter root vegetables together for a wonderfully warming and satisfying soup.

INGREDIENTS

Serves 6

3 carrots, chopped
1 large potato, chopped
1 large parsnip, chopped
1 large turnip or small swede
   (rutabaga), chopped
1 onion, chopped
30ml/2 tbsp sunflower oil
25g/1oz/2 tbsp butter
1.5 litres/2½ pints/6¼ cups Vegetable
   Stock or water
1 piece fresh root ginger, grated
300ml/½ pint/1¼ cups milk
45ml/3 tbsp crème fraîche or fromage
   frais
30ml/2 tbsp chopped fresh dill
15ml/1 tbsp lemon juice
salt and ground black pepper
fresh dill sprigs, to garnish

1 Put the carrots, potato, parsnip, turnip or swede and onion into a large pan with the oil and butter. Cook lightly, then cover and sweat the vegetables over a low heat for 15 minutes, shaking the pan occasionally.

2 Pour in the stock or water, bring to the boil and season to taste with salt and pepper. Cover and simmer for 20 minutes until the vegetables are soft.

3 Strain the vegetables, reserving the cooking liquid, add the ginger and vegetables to a food processor or blender and process until smooth. Return the puréed mixture and cooking liquid to the pan. Add the milk and stir while the soup gently reheats.

4 Remove the pan from the heat and stir in the crème fraîche or fromage frais, plus the dill and lemon juice. Taste and adjust the seasoning if necessary. Reheat the soup, but do not allow it to boil or it may curdle. Serve garnished with sprigs of dill.

BEAN, LENTIL
& CHICKPEA
SOUPS

Celeriac and Spinach Soup

Celeriac has a wonderful flavour that is reminiscent of celery, but also adds a slightly nutty taste. Here, it is combined with spinach to make a delicious soup.

INGREDIENTS

Serves 6

1 litre/1¾ pints/4 cups water

250ml/8fl oz/1 cup dry white wine

1 leek, thickly sliced

500g/1¼lb celeriac, diced

200g/7 oz fresh spinach leaves

freshly grated nutmeg

salt and ground black pepper

25g/1oz/¼ cup pine nuts,
   to garnish

1 Mix the water and wine in a jug (pitcher). Place the leek, celeriac and spinach in a deep pan and pour the liquid over the top. Bring to the boil, lower the heat and simmer for 10–15 minutes, until the vegetables are soft.

2 Pour the celeriac mixture into a blender or food processor and process until smooth, in batches if necessary. Return to the clean pan and season to taste with salt, pepper and grated nutmeg. Reheat gently.

3 Heat a non-stick frying pan (do not add any oil) and add the pine nuts. Dry-fry until golden brown, stirring occasionally so that they do not stick. Sprinkle them over the soup and serve.

COOK'S TIP

If the soup is too thick, thin with a little water or semi-skimmed (low-fat) milk when processing.

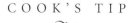

Star-gazer Vegetable Soup

For a different flavour, you could also make this soup with chicken or fish stock. All are equally tasty and the soup makes an attractive first course for a dinner party.

INGREDIENTS

Serves 4

1 yellow (bell) pepper

2 large courgettes (zucchini)

2 large carrots

1 kohlrabi

900ml/1½ pints/3¾ cups Vegetable Stock

50g/2oz rice vermicelli

salt and ground black pepper

1 Cut the pepper into quarters, removing the seeds and core. Cut the courgettes and carrots lengthways into 5 mm/¼in slices and slice the kohlrabi into 5 mm/¼in rounds.

2 Using tiny pastry (cookie) cutters, stamp out shapes from the vegetables or use a very sharp knife to cut the slices into stars and other decorative shapes.

COOK'S TIP

Sauté the leftover vegetable pieces in a little oil and mix with cooked brown rice to make a tasty risotto.

3 Place the vegetables and stock in a pan and simmer for 10 minutes, until the vegetables are tender. Season to taste with salt and pepper.

4 Meanwhile, place the rice vermicelli in a bowl, cover with boiling water and set aside for 4 minutes. Drain, then divide among four warmed soup bowls. Ladle the soup over the rice vermicelli and serve immediately.

Spicy Carrot Soup with Garlic Croûtons

Carrot soup is given a touch of spice with coriander, cumin and chilli powder.

INGREDIENTS

Serves 6

15ml/l tbsp olive oil

1 large onion, chopped

675g/1½ lb carrots, sliced

5ml/1 tsp ground coriander

5ml/1 tsp ground cumin

5ml/1 tsp hot chilli powder

900ml/1½ pints/3¾ cups Vegetable Stock

salt and ground black pepper

fresh coriander (cilantro) sprigs, to garnish

For the garlic croûtons

4 slices bread, crusts removed

a little olive oil

2 garlic cloves, crushed

1 To make the soup, heat the oil in a large pan, add the onion and carrots and cook over a low heat for 5 minutes, stirring occasionally. Add the ground spices and cook gently for 1 minute, stirring constantly.

2 Stir in the stock, bring to the boil, then cover and simmer gently for about 45 minutes, until the carrots are tender.

3 Meanwhile, make the garlic croûtons. Cut the bread into 1cm/½in cubes. Heat the oil in a frying pan, add the garlic and cook gently for 30 seconds, stirring constantly. Add the bread cubes, turn them over in the oil and fry over a medium heat for a few minutes, until they are crisp and golden brown all over, turning frequently. Drain on kitchen paper and keep warm.

4 Process the soup in a blender or food processor until smooth, then season to taste with salt and pepper. Return the soup to the rinsed pan and reheat gently. Serve hot, sprinkled with garlic croûtons and garnished with fresh coriander sprigs.

Minestrone with Pesto

In Genoa, they often make minestrone like this, with fresh pesto stirred in towards the end of cooking. It is packed full of vegetables and has a strong, heady flavour, making it an excellent vegetarian dish. There is Parmesan cheese in the pesto, so there is no need to serve any extra with the soup.

INGREDIENTS

Serves 4–6

45ml/3 tbsp olive oil

1 onion, finely chopped

2 celery sticks, finely chopped

1 large carrot, finely chopped

150g/5oz green beans, cut into 5cm/
    2in pieces

1 courgette (zucchini), thinly sliced

1 potato, cut into 1cm/½in cubes

¼ Savoy cabbage, shredded

1 small aubergine (eggplant), cut into
    1cm/½in cubes

200g/7oz can cannellini beans, drained
    and rinsed

2 Italian plum tomatoes, chopped

1.2 litres/2 pints/5 cups Vegetable Stock

90g/3½oz dried spaghetti or vermicelli

salt and ground black pepper

For the pesto

about 20 fresh basil leaves

1 garlic clove

10ml/2 tsp pine nuts

15ml/1 tbsp freshly grated
    Parmesan cheese

15ml/1 tbsp freshly grated
    Pecorino cheese

30ml/2 tbsp olive oil

1 Heat the oil in a large, heavy pan, add the chopped onion, celery and carrot, and cook over a low heat, stirring frequently, for 5–7 minutes.

2 Mix in the green beans, courgette, potato and Savoy cabbage. Stir-fry over a medium heat for about 3 minutes. Add the aubergine, cannellini beans and plum tomatoes and stir-fry for 2–3 minutes.

3 Pour in the stock and season with salt and pepper to taste. Bring to the boil. Stir well, cover and lower the heat. Simmer for 40 minutes, stirring occasionally.

4 Meanwhile, process all the pesto ingredients in a food processor until the mixture forms a smooth sauce, adding 15–45ml/ 1–3 tbsp water through the feeder tube if the sauce seems too thick.

5 Break the pasta into small pieces and add it to the soup. Simmer, stirring frequently, for 5 minutes. Add the pesto sauce and stir it in well, then simmer for 2–3 minutes more, or until the pasta is *al dente*. Check the seasoning and serve hot, in warmed soup plates or bowls.

Curried Carrot and Apple Soup

The combination of carrot, curry and apple is a highly successful one. Curried fruit is delicious.

INGREDIENTS

Serves 4

10ml/2 tsp sunflower oil

15ml/1 tbsp mild korma curry powder

500g/1¼lb carrots, chopped

1 large onion, chopped

1 large cooking apple, chopped

750ml/1¼ pints/3 cups Chicken Stock

salt and ground black pepper

natural (plain) yogurt and carrot curls, to garnish

3 Cook over a low heat for about 15 minutes, shaking the pan occasionally, until the vegetables are softened. Spoon the vegetable mixture into a food processor or blender, add half the stock and process until smooth.

4 Return the mixture to the pan and pour in the remaining chicken stock. Bring the soup to the boil, then taste and adjust the seasoning. Ladle into warm bowls and serve, garnished with a swirl of yogurt and curls of raw carrot.

1 Heat the oil in a large, heavy pan and gently cook the curry powder for 2–3 minutes.

2 Add the chopped carrots and onion and the cooking apple, stir well until coated with the curry powder, then cover the pan.

Roasted Tomato and Pasta Soup

When the only tomatoes you can buy are not particularly flavoursome, make this soup. The roasting compensates for any lack of flavour in the tomatoes, and the soup has a wonderful, smoky taste.

INGREDIENTS

Serves 4

450g/1lb ripe Italian plum tomatoes, halved lengthways

1 large red (bell) pepper, quartered lengthways and seeded

1 large red onion, quartered lengthways

2 garlic cloves, unpeeled

15ml/1 tbsp olive oil

1.2 litres/2 pints/5 cups Vegetable Stock or water

good pinch of granulated sugar

90g/3½oz/scant 1 cup small dried pasta shapes, such as tubetti

salt and ground black pepper

fresh basil leaves, to garnish

1 Preheat the oven to 190°C/375°F/Gas 5. Spread out the tomatoes, red pepper, onion and garlic in a roasting pan and drizzle with the olive oil. Roast for 30–40 minutes, until the vegetables are soft and charred, stirring and turning them halfway through cooking.

2 Tip the vegetables into a food processor, add about 250ml/8fl oz/1 cup of the stock or water, and process to a purée. Scrape into a sieve placed over a large pan and press the purée through with the back of a spoon into the pan.

3 Add the remaining stock or water, the sugar and salt and pepper to taste. Bring to the boil.

4 Add the pasta and simmer for 7–8 minutes (or according to the instructions on the packet), stirring frequently, until *al dente*. Taste and adjust the seasoning with salt and ground black pepper, if necessary. Serve immediately in warmed bowls, garnished with the fresh basil leaves.

COOK'S TIP

You can roast the vegetables in advance, leave them to cool, then store them in a covered bowl in the refrigerator overnight before puréeing.

Leek, Parsnip and Ginger Soup

A flavoursome winter warmer, with the added spiciness of fresh ginger, this unusual soup is destined to become a family favourite.

INGREDIENTS

Serves 4–6

30ml/2 tbsp olive oil

225g/8oz leeks, sliced

25g/1oz fresh root ginger, finely chopped

675g/1½lb parsnips, coarsely chopped

300ml/½ pint/1¼ cups dry white wine

1.2 litres/2 pints/5 cups Vegetable Stock
   or water

salt and ground black pepper

fromage blanc and paprika,
   to garnish

1 Heat the oil in a large pan and add the leeks and ginger. Cook gently for 2–3 minutes, until the leeks start to soften.

2 Add the parsnips and cook for a further 7–8 minutes, until they are beginning to soften.

3 Pour in the wine and stock or water and bring to the boil. Reduce the heat and simmer gently for 20–30 minutes, or until the parsnips are tender. Leave the soup to cool slightly.

4 Process the soup in a blender or food processor until smooth. Season to taste with salt and pepper. Reheat and garnish with a swirl of fromage blanc and a light dusting of paprika.

Tortellini Chanterelle Broth

The savoury-sweet quality of chanterelle mushrooms combines well in a simple broth with spinach-and-ricotta-filled tortellini. The addition of a little sherry creates a lovely warming effect.

INGREDIENTS

Serves 4

350g/12oz fresh spinach and ricotta tortellini, or 175g/6oz dried

1.2 litres/2 pints/5 cups Chicken Stock

75ml/5 tbsp dry sherry

175g/6oz fresh chanterelle mushrooms, trimmed and sliced, or 15g/¹/₂oz/¹/₂ cup dried chanterelles

chopped fresh parsley, to garnish

1 Cook the tortellini according to the packet instructions.

2 Bring the chicken stock to the boil, add the dry sherry and fresh or dried mushrooms and simmer for 10 minutes.

3 Strain the tortellini, add to the stock, then ladle the broth into four warmed soup bowls, making sure each contains the same proportions of tortellini and mushrooms. Garnish with the chopped parsley and serve.

C H U N K Y
V E G E T A B L E
S O U P S

Beetroot Soup with Ravioli

Beetroot and pasta make an unusual combination, but this soup is no less good for that.

INGREDIENTS

Serves 4–6

12 sheets of fresh lasagne

1 egg white, beaten, for brushing

plain (all-purpose) flour, for dusting

1 small onion or shallot, finely chopped

2 garlic cloves, crushed

5ml/1 tsp fennel seeds

600ml/1 pint/2½ cups Chicken or
    Vegetable Stock

225g/8oz cooked beetroot (beet)

30ml/2 tbsp fresh orange juice

fresh fennel or dill leaves, to garnish

crusty bread, to serve

For the filling

115g/4oz mushrooms, finely chopped

1 shallot or small onion, finely chopped

1–2 garlic cloves, crushed

5ml/1 tsp chopped fresh thyme

15ml/1 tbsp chopped fresh parsley

90ml/6 tbsp fresh white breadcrumbs

salt and ground black pepper

large pinch of freshly grated nutmeg

1 Put all the filling ingredients in a food processor or blender and process to a paste.

2 Lightly mark six squares on a lasagne sheet. Put 5ml/1 tsp of the filling on each square. Brush around the edges of each square with egg white. Cover with another lasagne sheet and seal the edges. Cut into six squares. Repeat with the other lasagne sheets and the remaining filling. Leave to rest for 1 hour before cooking.

3 Cook the ravioli salted, boiling water for 2 minutes. (Cook in batches to stop them sticking together.) Remove and drop into a bowl of cold water for 5 seconds before placing on a tray. (You can make the ravioli a day in advance and store in the refrigerator.)

4 Put the onion, garlic and fennel seeds into a pan with 150ml/¼ pint/⅔ cup of the stock. Bring to the boil, cover and simmer for 5 minutes, until tender. Peel and finely dice the beetroot, reserving 60ml/4 tbsp for the garnish. Add the rest of it to the soup with the remaining stock, and bring to the boil.

5 Add the orange juice and cooked ravioli and simmer for 2 minutes. Serve in shallow soup bowls, garnished with the reserved diced beetroot and fresh fennel or dill leaves. Serve hot, with crusty bread.

Green Pea Soup with Spinach

This lovely green soup was invented by the wife of a seventeenth-century British Member of Parliament, and it has stood the test of time.

INGREDIENTS

Serves 6

450g/1lb/generous 3 cups podded fresh or
    frozen peas

1 leek, finely sliced

2 garlic cloves, crushed

2 rindless back (lean) bacon rashers,
    finely diced

1.2 litres/2 pints/5 cups Chicken Stock

30ml/2 tbsp olive oil

50g/2 oz fresh spinach, shredded

40g/1½oz/⅓ cup white cabbage,
    finely shredded

½ small lettuce, finely shredded

1 celery stick, finely chopped

large handful of parsley, finely chopped

½ carton mustard and cress

20ml/4 tsp chopped fresh mint

pinch of ground mace

salt and ground black pepper

1 Put the peas, leek, garlic and bacon in a large pan. Add the chicken stock, bring to the boil, then lower the heat and simmer for 20 minutes.

2 About 5 minutes before the pea mixture is ready, heat the oil in a deep frying pan.

3 Add the spinach, cabbage, lettuce, celery and herbs to the frying pan. Cover and sweat the mixture over a low heat until soft.

4 Transfer the pea mixture to a blender or food processor and process until smooth. Return to the clean pan, add the sweated vegetables and herbs and heat through. Season with mace, salt and pepper and serve.

Pasta Squares and Peas in Broth

This thick soup is from Lazio, the region around Rome, where it is traditionally made with fresh home-made pasta and peas. In this modern version, ready-made pasta is used with frozen peas to save time.

INGREDIENTS

Serves 4–6

25g/1oz/2 tbsp butter

50g/2oz/⅓ cup pancetta or rindless smoked streaky (fatty) bacon, coarsely chopped

1 small onion, finely chopped

1 celery stick, finely chopped

400g/14oz/3½ cups frozen peas

5ml/1 tsp tomato purée (paste)

5–10ml/1–2 tsp finely chopped fresh flat leaf parsley

1 litre/1¾ pints/4 cups Chicken Stock

300g/11oz fresh lasagne sheets

about 50g/2oz/⅓ cup prosciutto, diced

salt and ground black pepper

grated Parmesan cheese, to serve

1 Melt the butter in a large pan and add the pancetta or bacon, with the onion and celery. Cook over a low heat, stirring constantly, for 5 minutes.

COOK'S TIP
～

Take care when adding salt because of the saltiness of the pancetta and the prosciutto.

2 Add the peas and cook, stirring, for 3–4 minutes. Stir in the tomato purée and parsley, then add the stock, with salt and pepper to taste. Bring to the boil. Cover the pan, lower the heat and simmer gently for 10 minutes. Meanwhile, cut the lasagne sheets into 2cm/¾in squares.

3 Taste the soup and adjust the seasoning if necessary. Drop in the pasta, stir and bring to the boil. Simmer for 2–3 minutes, or until the pasta is *al dente*, then stir in the prosciutto. Ladle the soup into warmed bowls and serve hot, with grated Parmesan cheese handed around separately.

Leek and Thyme Soup

This heart-warming soup can be processed to a smooth purée or served in its original peasant style.

INGREDIENTS

Serves 4

900g/2lb leeks

450g/1lb potatoes

115g/4oz/½ cup butter

1 large fresh thyme sprig, plus extra to garnish (optional)

300ml/½ pint/1¼ cups milk

salt and ground black pepper

60ml/4 tbsp double (heavy) cream, to serve

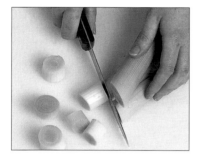

1 Trim the leeks. If you are using large winter leeks, strip away all the coarse outer leaves, then cut the leeks into thick slices. Wash thoroughly under cold running water to remove any traces of soil.

2 Cut the potatoes into coarse dice, about 2.5cm/1in, and dry on kitchen paper.

3 Melt the butter in a large pan and add the leeks and 1 sprig of thyme. Cover and cook for 4–5 minutes, until softened. Add the potato pieces and just enough cold water to cover the vegetables. Re-cover and cook over a low heat for 30 minutes.

4 Pour in the milk and season to taste with salt and pepper. Cover and simmer for a further 30 minutes. You will find that some of the potato breaks up, leaving you with a semi-puréed and rather lumpy soup.

5 Remove the sprig of thyme (the leaves will have fallen into the soup) and serve, adding 15ml/1 tbsp cream and a garnish of thyme to each portion, if using.

Courgette Soup with Pasta

This is a pretty, fresh-tasting soup, which is always a welcome dish in hot weather.

INGREDIENTS

Serves 4–6

60 ml/4 tbsp olive or sunflower oil

2 onions, finely chopped

1.5 litres/2½ pints/6¼ cups chicken stock

900 g/2 1b courgettes (zucchini)

115 g/4 oz small soup pasta (stellette)

a little lemon juice

30 ml/2 tbsp chopped fresh chervil

salt and freshly ground black pepper

sour cream, to serve

1 Heat the oil in a large saucepan and add the onions. Cover and cook gently for about 20 minutes, stirring occasionally, until soft but not coloured.

2 Add the stock to the pan and bring the mixture to the boil.

3 Meanwhile, grate the courgettes and stir into the boiling stock with the pasta. Reduce the heat, cover the pan and simmer for 15 minutes until the pasta is tender.

4 Season to taste with lemon juice, salt and pepper. Stir in the chopped fresh chervil. Pour into bowls and add a swirl of sour cream before serving.

VARIATION

You can use cucumber instead of courgettes, if you prefer, and other soup pasta such as tiny shells.

Spinach and Rice Soup

Use very fresh, young spinach leaves and risotto rice to prepare this surprisingly light, refreshing soup.

INGREDIENTS

Serves 4

675g/1½lb fresh spinach, washed
45ml/3 tbsp extra virgin olive oil
1 small onion, finely chopped
2 garlic cloves, finely chopped
1 small fresh red chilli, seeded and
    finely chopped
115g/4oz/generous ½ cup risotto rice
1.2 litres/2 pints/5 cups Vegetable Stock
salt and ground black pepper
60ml/4 tbsp grated Pecorino cheese,
    to serve

1 Place the spinach in a large pan with just the water that clings to its leaves after washing. Add a large pinch of salt. Heat gently until the spinach has wilted, then remove from the heat and drain, reserving any liquid. Use a knife to chop finely.

2 Heat the oil in a large pan and cook the onion, garlic and chilli over a medium heat, stirring occasionally, for 4–5 minutes, until softened. Stir in the rice until well coated, then pour in the stock and reserved spinach liquid.

3 Bring to the boil, lower the heat and simmer gently for 10 minutes. Add the spinach and cook for 5–7 minutes more, until the rice is tender. Season with salt and freshly ground pepper to taste and serve immediately with the Pecorino cheese.

Chunky Vegetable Soups

Chicken Stellette Soup

Simple and quick to prepare, provided you have some good stock to hand, this light, clear soup is easy on the palate and the eye.

INGREDIENTS

Serves 4–6

900 ml/1½ pints/3¾ cups chicken stock

1 bay leaf

4 spring onions (scallions), sliced

225 g/8 oz button (white) mushrooms, sliced

115 g/4 oz cooked chicken breast portion

50 g/2 oz small soup pasta (stellette)

150 ml/¼ pint/⅔ cup dry white wine

15 ml/1 tbsp chopped parsley

salt and freshly ground black pepper

1 Put the stock and bay leaf into a large pan and bring to the boil. Add the sliced spring onions and mushrooms.

2 Remove the skin from the chicken and discard. Slice the chicken thinly, add to the soup and season to taste with salt and pepper. Heat through for 2–3 minutes.

3 Add the pasta to the soup, cover and simmer for 7–8 minutes until the pasta is *al dente*.

4 Just before serving, add the wine and chopped parsley and heat through for 2–3 minutes. Pour in to individual soup bowls.

Chinese Tofu and Lettuce Soup

This light, clear soup is brimful of colourful, tasty vegetables.

INGREDIENTS

Serves 4

30 ml/2 tbsp groundnut (peanut) oil

200 g/7 oz smoked or marinated tofu, cubed

3 spring onions (scallions), sliced diagonally

2 garlic cloves, cut into thin strips

1 carrot, finely sliced into rounds

1 litre/1¾ pints/4 cups vegetable stock

30 ml/2 tbsp soy sauce

15 ml/l tbsp dry sherry or vermouth

5 ml/1 tsp sugar

115 g/4 oz Cos (romaine) lettuce, shredded

salt and freshly ground black pepper

1 Heat the oil in a preheated wok, then stir-fry the tofu cubes until browned. Drain on kitchen paper and set aside.

2 Add the spring onions, garlic and carrot to the wok and stir-fry for 2 minutes. Add the stock, soy sauce, sherry or vermouth, sugar, lettuce and fried tofu. Heat through gently for 1 minute, season to taste and serve.

Chicken Soup with Vermicelli

In Morocco, the cook – who is almost invariably the most senior woman of the household – would use a whole chicken for this tasty and nourishing soup, to serve to her large extended family.

INGREDIENTS

Serves 4–6

30ml/2 tbsp sunflower oil

15g/¹⁄₂oz/1 tbsp butter

1 onion, chopped

2 chicken legs or breast portions, halved or quartered

plain (all-purpose) flour, for dusting

2 carrots, cut into 4cm/1¹⁄₂in pieces

1 parsnip, cut into 4cm/1¹⁄₂in pieces

1.5 litres/2¹⁄₂ pints/6¹⁄₄ cups Chicken Stock

1 cinnamon stick

good pinch of paprika

pinch of saffron threads

2 egg yolks

juice of ¹⁄₂ lemon

30ml/2 tbsp chopped fresh coriander (cilantro)

30ml/2 tbsp chopped fresh parsley

150g/5 oz dried vermicelli

salt and ground black pepper

1 Heat the oil and butter in a pan and cook the onion for 3–4 minutes, until softened. Dust the chicken pieces in seasoned flour and cook gently until they are evenly browned.

2 Transfer the chicken to a plate and add the carrots and parsnip to the pan. Cook over a low heat for 3–4 minutes, stirring frequently, then return the chicken to the pan. Add the chicken stock, cinnamon stick and paprika and season well with salt and pepper.

3 Bring the soup to the boil, cover and simmer for 1 hour, until the vegetables are very tender.

4 Meanwhile, blend the saffron in 30ml/2 tbsp boiling water. Beat the egg yolks with the lemon juice in a separate bowl and add the coriander and parsley. When the saffron water has cooled, stir into the egg and lemon mixture.

5 When the vegetables are tender, transfer the chicken to a plate. Spoon away any excess fat from the soup, then increase the heat a little and stir in the vermicelli. Cook for a further 5–6 minutes, until the pasta is *al dente*. Meanwhile, remove the skin and bones from the chicken and chop the flesh into bitesize pieces.

6 When the vermicelli is cooked, stir in the chicken pieces and the egg yolk, lemon and saffron mixture. Cook over a low heat for 1–2 minutes, stirring constantly. Adjust the seasoning and serve.

Apple Soup

A delicious soup that makes the most of freshly picked apples.

INGREDIENTS

Serves 6

45ml/3 tbsp oil

1 kohlrabi, diced

3 carrots, diced

2 celery sticks, diced

1 green (bell) pepper, seeded and diced

2 tomatoes, diced

2 litres/3½ pints/9 cups Chicken Stock

6 large green apples

45ml/3 tbsp plain (all-purpose) flour

150ml/¼ pint/⅔ cup double (heavy) cream

15ml/1 tbsp granulated sugar

30–45ml/2–3 tbsp lemon juice

salt and ground black pepper

lemon wedges and crusty bread, to serve

1 Heat the oil in a large pan. Add the kohlrabi, carrots, celery, green pepper and tomatoes and cook, stirring occasionally, for 5–6 minutes, until just softened.

2 Pour in the chicken stock, bring to the boil, then reduce the heat and simmer for about 45 minutes.

3 Meanwhile, peel and core the apples, then chop into small cubes. Add to the pan and simmer for a further 15 minutes.

4 In a bowl, mix together the flour and cream, then pour slowly into the soup, stirring well, and bring to the boil. Add the sugar and lemon juice before seasoning. Serve immediately with lemon wedges and crusty bread.

Pasta Soup with Chicken Livers

*The fried chicken livers in this dish
are so delicious that, even if you do
not normally like them, you will
find yourself lapping them up with
enthusiasm in this soup.*

INGREDIENTS

Serves 4–6

115g/4oz/¹/₂ cup chicken livers, thawed
    if frozen

15ml/1 tbsp olive oil

knob (pat) of butter

4 garlic cloves, crushed

3 sprigs each of fresh parsley, marjoram
    and sage, chopped

1 fresh thyme sprig, chopped

5–6 fresh basil leaves, chopped

15–30ml/1–2 tbsp dry white wine

2 x 300g/11oz cans condensed
    chicken consommé

225g/8oz/2 cups frozen peas

50g/2oz/¹/₂ cup small dried pasta shapes,
    such as farfalle

2–3 spring onions (scallions),
    sliced diagonally

salt and ground black pepper

1 Cut the chicken livers into
   small pieces with scissors.
Heat the oil and butter in a frying
pan, add the garlic and herbs, with
salt and ground black pepper to
taste, and cook gently for a few
minutes. Add the livers, increase
the heat to high and stir-fry for a
few minutes until they change
colour and become dry. Add the
wine, cook until it evaporates,
then remove from the heat.

2 Tip both cans of chicken
   consommé into a large pan
and add water to the condensed
soup as directed on the labels. Add
an extra can of water, then stir in a
little salt and pepper to taste and
bring to the boil.

3 Add the frozen peas to the
   pan and simmer for about
5 minutes, then add the small pasta
shapes and bring the soup back to
the boil, stirring constantly. Lower
the heat and gently simmer the
soup, stirring frequently, for about
5 minutes, or according to the
instructions on the packet, until
the pasta is *al dente*.

4 Add the fried chicken livers
   and spring onions and heat
through for 2–3 minutes. Taste and
adjust the seasoning if necessary.
Serve hot, in warmed bowls.

Beetroot and Apricot Swirl

This soup is most attractive if you swirl together the two differently coloured mixtures, but if you prefer they can be mixed together to save on both time and washing up.

INGREDIENTS

Serves 4

4 large cooked beetroots (beets), roughly chopped

1 small onion, roughly chopped

600 ml/1 pint/2½ cups chicken stock

200 g/7 oz/1 cup ready-to-eat dried apricots

250 ml/8 fl oz/1 cup orange juice

salt and freshly ground black pepper

2 Place the rest of the onion in a pan with the apricots and orange juice, cover and simmer gently for about 15 minutes, until tender. Purée in a food processor or blender.

3 Return the two mixtures to the saucepans and reheat. Season to taste with salt and pepper, then swirl them together in individual soup bowls for a marbled effect.

1 Place the roughly chopped beetroot and half the onion in a pan with the stock. Bring to the boil, then reduce the heat, cover and simmer for about 10 minutes. Place the mixture in a food processor or blender and purée until smooth.

COOK'S TIP

The apricot mixture should be the same consistency as the beetroot mixture – if it is too thick, add a little more orange juice.

Meatball and Pasta Soup

This soup, which comes from sunny Sicily, is a substantial primo – a first course that in Italy is considered as important as the second.

Serves 4

2 x 300g/11oz cans condensed
   beef consommé
90g/3¹/₂oz/³/₄ cup very thin dried pasta,
   such as fidelini or spaghettini
chopped fresh flat leaf parsley, to garnish
grated Parmesan cheese, to serve

For the meatballs

1 very thick slice white bread,
   crusts removed
30ml/2 tbsp milk
225g/8oz/1 cup minced (ground) beef
1 garlic clove, crushed
30ml/2 tbsp grated Parmesan cheese
30–45ml/2–3 tbsp fresh flat leaf parsley
   leaves, coarsely chopped
1 egg
generous pinch of freshly grated nutmeg
salt and ground black pepper

1 Make the meatballs. Break the bread into a small bowl, add the milk and set aside to soak. Meanwhile, put the minced beef, garlic, Parmesan, parsley and egg in another large bowl. Grate the nutmeg liberally over the top and add salt and pepper to taste.

2 Squeeze the bread with your hands to remove as much milk as possible, then add the bread to the meatball mixture and mix everything together well with your hands. Wash your hands, rinse them under cold water, then form the mixture into tiny balls about the size of small marbles.

3 Tip both cans of consommé into a large pan, add water as directed on the labels, then add an extra can of water. Season to taste with salt and pepper, bring to the boil and add the meatballs.

4 Break the pasta into small pieces and add it to the soup. Bring to the boil, stirring gently. Simmer, stirring frequently, for 7–8 minutes or according to the instructions on the packet, until the pasta is *al dente*. Taste and adjust the seasoning.

5 Ladle into warmed bowls and serve immediately, garnished with chopped parsley and freshly grated Parmesan cheese.

Pistou

Serve this delicious vegetable soup from Nice, in the south of France, with a sun-dried tomato pesto and fresh Parmesan cheese.

Serves 4

1 courgette (zucchini), diced

1 small potato, diced

1 shallot, chopped

1 carrot, diced

225g/8oz can chopped tomatoes

1.2 litres/2 pints/5 cups Vegetable Stock

50g/2oz green beans, cut into 1cm/
  ¹⁄₂in lengths

50g/2oz/¹⁄₂ cup petits pois (baby peas)

50g/2oz/¹⁄₂ cup small pasta shapes

60–90ml/4–6 tbsp pesto, either
  home-made or ready-made

15ml/1 tbsp sun-dried tomato paste

salt and ground black pepper

grated Parmesan cheese, to serve

1 Place the courgette, potato, shallot, carrot and tomatoes in a large pan. Add the vegetable stock and season with salt and pepper. Bring to the boil, then cover and simmer for 20 minutes.

2 Add the green beans, petits pois and pasta shapes. Cook for a further 10 minutes, until the pasta is tender.

3 Taste the soup and adjust the seasoning as necessary. Ladle the soup into individual bowls. Mix together the pesto and sun-dried tomato paste, and stir a spoonful into each serving.

4 Hand round a bowl of grated Parmesan cheese for sprinkling into each bowl.

Clam and Pasta Soup

This soup is a variation of the pasta dish spaghetti alle vongole, *using store-cupboard ingredients. Serve it with hot focaccia or ciabatta for a filling first course.*

INGREDIENTS

Serves 4

30ml/2 tbsp olive oil

1 large onion, finely chopped

2 garlic cloves, crushed

400g/14oz can chopped tomatoes

15ml/1 tbsp sun-dried tomato paste

5ml/1 tsp granulated sugar

5ml/1 tsp dried mixed herbs

about 750ml/1¼ pints/3 cups Fish or
    Vegetable Stock

150ml/¼ pint/⅔ cup red wine

50g/2oz/½ cup small dried pasta shapes

150g/5oz jar or can clams in natural juice

30ml/2 tbsp finely chopped fresh flat leaf
    parsley, plus a few whole leaves
    to garnish

salt and ground black pepper

1 Heat the oil in a large, heavy pan. Add the onion and cook gently for 5 minutes, stirring frequently, until softened.

2 Add the garlic, tomatoes, sun-dried tomato paste, sugar, herbs, stock and wine and season with salt and pepper to taste. Bring to the boil. Lower the heat, half-cover the pan and simmer, stirring occasionally, for 10 minutes.

3 Add the pasta and continue simmering, uncovered, for about 10 minutes, or until the pasta is *al dente.* Stir occasionally to prevent the pasta shapes from sticking together.

4 Add the clams and their juice to the soup and heat through for 3–4 minutes, adding more stock if required. Do not allow it to boil, or the clams will become tough. Remove from the heat, stir in the chopped parsley and adjust the seasoning. Serve hot, sprinkled with coarsely ground black pepper and parsley leaves.

Summer Vegetable Soup

This brightly coloured, fresh-tasting soup makes the most of summer's vegetable crop.

INGREDIENTS

Serves 4

45ml/3 tbsp olive oil

1 large onion, finely chopped

15ml/1 tbsp sun-dried tomato paste

450g/1lb ripe Italian plum tomatoes, peeled and finely chopped

225g/8oz green courgettes (zucchini), trimmed and coarsely chopped

225g/8oz yellow courgettes (zucchini), trimmed and coarsely chopped

3 waxy new potatoes, diced

2 garlic cloves, crushed

about 1.2 litres/2 pints/5 cups Vegetable Stock or water

60ml/4 tbsp shredded fresh basil

50g/2oz/⅔ cup grated Parmesan cheese

salt and ground black pepper

1 Heat the oil in a large pan, add the onion and cook over a low heat for about 5 minutes, stirring constantly, until softened.

2 Stir in the sun-dried tomato paste, chopped tomatoes, courgettes, diced potatoes and garlic. Mix well and cook gently for 10 minutes, uncovered, shaking the pan frequently to stop the vegetables sticking to the base.

3 Pour in the stock or water. Bring to the boil, lower the heat, half-cover the pan and simmer gently for 15 minutes, or until the vegetables are just tender. Add more stock if necessary.

4 Remove the pan from the heat and stir in the basil and half the cheese. Taste and adjust the seasoning. Serve hot, sprinkled with the remaining cheese.

Broccoli, Anchovy and Pasta Soup

This soup is from Apulia in the
south of Italy, where anchovies and
broccoli are often used together.

INGREDIENTS

Serves 4

30ml/2 tbsp olive oil

1 small onion, finely chopped

1 garlic clove, finely chopped

¼–⅓ fresh red chilli, seeded and
   finely chopped

2 canned anchovy fillets, drained

200ml/7fl oz/scant 1 cup passata (bottled
   strained tomatoes)

45ml/3 tbsp dry white wine

1.2 litres/2 pints/5 cups Vegetable Stock

300g/11oz/2 cups broccoli florets

200g/7oz/1¾ cups dried orecchiette

salt and ground black pepper

grated Pecorino cheese, to serve

1 Heat the oil in a large pan.
Add the onion, garlic, chilli
and anchovies and cook over a
low heat, stirring constantly, for
5–6 minutes.

2 Add the passata and white
wine and season with salt and
pepper to taste. Bring to the boil,
cover the pan, then cook over a
low heat, stirring occasionally, for
12–15 minutes.

3 Pour in the vegetable stock.
Bring to the boil, then add the
broccoli and simmer for about
5 minutes. Add the pasta and bring
back to the boil, stirring constantly.
Simmer for 7–8 minutes, or
according to the instructions on the
packet, stirring frequently, until the
pasta is *al dente*.

4 Taste and adjust the seasoning.
Serve hot, in individual
warmed bowls. Hand round the
grated Pecorino cheese separately.

Italian Rocket and Potato Soup

This filling and hearty soup is based on a traditional Italian peasant recipe. If rocket is unavailable, watercress or baby spinach leaves make an equally delicious alternative.

INGREDIENTS

Serves 4

900g/2lb new potatoes

900ml/1½ pints/3¾ cups Vegetable Stock

1 carrot

115g/4oz rocket (arugula)

2.5ml/½ tsp cayenne pepper

½ loaf stale ciabatta bread, torn
    into chunks

4 garlic cloves, thinly sliced

60ml/4 tbsp olive oil

salt and ground black pepper

3 Add the cayenne pepper, plus salt and black pepper to taste, then add the chunks of bread. Remove the pan from the heat, cover and leave to stand for about 10 minutes.

4 Meanwhile, sauté the garlic in the olive oil until golden brown. Pour the soup into bowls, add a little of the sautéed garlic to each bowl and serve.

1 Dice the potatoes, then place them in a pan with the stock and a little salt. Bring to the boil and simmer for 10 minutes.

2 Finely dice the carrot and add to the potatoes and stock, then tear the rocket leaves and drop into the pan. Simmer for a further 15 minutes, until the vegetables are tender.

PASTA &
NOODLE
SOUPS

Winter Vegetable Soup

No fewer than eight varieties of vegetables are packed into this hearty and nutritious soup.

INGREDIENTS

Serves 8

1 medium Savoy cabbage, quartered
  and cored
30 ml/2 tbsp corn oil
4 carrots, finely sliced
2 celery stalks, finely sliced
2 parsnips, diced
1.5 litres/2½ pints/6¼ cups chicken stock
3 medium potatoes, diced
2 courgettes (zucchini), sliced
1 small red pepper, seeded and diced
115 g/4 oz/2 cups cauliflower florets
2 tomatoes, seeded and diced
2.5 ml/½ tsp fresh thyme leaves or
  ¼ tsp dried thyme
30 ml/2 tbsp chopped fresh parsley
salt and freshly ground black pepper

1 Using a sharp knife, slice the cabbage quarters into thin strips across the leaves.

2 Heat the oil in a large pan. Add the cabbage, carrots, celery and parsnips and cook for 10–15 minutes over medium heat, stirring frequently.

3 Stir the stock into the vegetables and bring to the boil, skimming off any foam that rises to the surface.

4 Add the potatoes, courgettes, pepper, cauliflower and tomatoes with the herbs, and salt and pepper to taste. Bring back to the boil. Reduce the heat to low, cover the pan and simmer for 15–20 minutes until the vegetables are tender. Serve hot.

Japanese Crushed Tofu Soup

*The main ingredient for this soup
is crushed tofu, which is both
nutritious and satisfying.*

INGREDIENTS

Serves 4

150g/5oz fresh tofu, weighed
   without water

2 dried shiitake mushrooms

50g/2oz gobo

5ml/1 tsp rice vinegar

1/2 black or white konnyaku (about 115g/
   4oz)

30ml/2 tbsp sesame oil

115g/4oz mooli (daikon), thinly sliced

50g/2oz carrot, thinly sliced

750ml/1 1/4 pints/3 cups Stock for Japanese
   Soups or instant dashi

pinch of salt

30ml/2 tbsp sake or dry white wine

7.5ml/1 1/2 tsp mirin

45ml/3 tbsp white or red miso paste

dash of soy sauce

6 mangetouts (snow peas), trimmed,
   boiled and finely sliced, to garnish

1 Crush the tofu coarsely by
hand until it resembles lumpy
scrambled egg in texture – do not
crush it too finely.

2 Wrap the tofu in a clean
dishtowel and put it in a sieve,
then pour over plenty of boiling
water. Leave the tofu to drain
thoroughly for 10 minutes.

3 Soak the dried shiitake
mushrooms in lukewarm
water for 20 minutes, then drain
them. Remove their stems and cut
the caps into 4–6 pieces.

4 Use a vegetable brush to scrub
the skin off the gobo and slice
it into thin shavings. Soak the
shavings for 5 minutes in plenty
of cold water to which the rice
vinegar has been added to remove
any bitter taste. Drain.

5 Put the konnyaku in a small
pan and cover with water.
Bring to the boil, then drain and
cool. Tear the konnyaku into
2cm/3/4in lumps: do not use a
knife, as smooth cuts will prevent
it from absorbing flavour.

6 Heat the sesame oil in a deep
pan. Add all the shiitake
mushrooms, gobo, mooli, carrot
and konnyaku. Stir-fry for
1 minute, then add the tofu and
stir well.

7 Pour in the stock/dashi and
add the salt, sake or wine and
mirin. Bring to the boil. Skim the
broth and simmer it for 5 minutes.

8 In a small bowl, dissolve the
miso paste in a little of the
soup, then return it to the pan.
Simmer the soup gently for
10 minutes, until the vegetables
are soft. Add the soy sauce, then
remove from the heat. Serve
immediately in four bowls,
garnished with the mangetouts.

Spicy Peanut Soup

A thick and warming vegetable soup, flavoured with mild chilli and roasted peanuts.

INGREDIENTS

Serves 6

30ml/2 tbsp oil

1 large onion, finely chopped

2 garlic cloves, crushed

5ml/1 tsp mild chilli powder

2 red (bell) peppers, seeded and chopped

225g/8oz carrots, finely chopped

225g/8oz potatoes, finely chopped

3 celery sticks, sliced

900ml/1½ pints/3¾ cups Vegetable Stock

90ml/6 tbsp crunchy peanut butter

115g/4oz/⅔ cup corn kernels

salt and ground black pepper

coarsely chopped unsalted roasted
    peanuts, to garnish

1 Heat the oil in a large pan and cook the onion and garlic for about 3 minutes. Add the chilli powder and cook for a further 1 minute.

2 Add the red peppers, carrots, potatoes and celery. Stir well, then cook for a further 4 minutes, stirring occasionally.

3 Add the vegetable stock, followed by the peanut butter and corn kernels. Stir well until thoroughly combined.

4 Season to taste with salt and pepper. Bring to the boil, cover and simmer for about 20 minutes, until all the vegetables are tender. Taste and adjust the seasoning if necessary before serving, sprinkled with the chopped peanuts.

Balinese Vegetable Soup

Any seasonal vegetables can be used in this soup, which is known as Sayur Oelih.

INGREDIENTS

Serves 8

225 g/8 oz green beans

1.2 litres/2 pints/5 cups boiling water

400 ml/14fl oz/1²⁄₃ cups coconut milk

1 garlic clove

2 macadamia nuts or 4 almonds

1 cm/¹⁄₂ in cube shrimp paste

10–15 ml/2–3 tsp coriander seeds,
   dry-fried and ground

oil for frying

1 onion, finely sliced

2 duan salam or bay leaves

225 g/8 oz beansprouts

30 ml/2 tbsp lemon juice

salt

1 Top and tail the green beans and cut into small pieces. Cook the beans in the salted, boiling water for 3–4 minutes. Drain the beans and reserve the cooking water.

2 Spoon off 45–60 ml/3–4 tbsp of the cream from the top of the coconut milk and set aside.

3 Grind the garlic, nuts, shrimp paste and ground coriander to a paste in a food processor or with a pestle and mortar.

4 Heat the oil in a wok or pan and fry the onion until transparent. Remove from the pan and reserve. Fry the paste for 2 minutes without browning. Pour in the reserved bean cooking water and coconut milk. Bring to the boil and add the duan salam or bay leaves. Cook, uncovered, for 15–20 minutes.

5 Just before serving, add the beans, fried onion, beansprouts, reserved coconut cream and lemon juice. Taste and adjust the seasoning, if necessary. Serve at once.

Tamarind Soup with Peanuts and Vegetables

Known in Indonesia as Sayur Asam, *this is a colourful and refreshing soup from Jakarta with more than a hint of sharpness.*

INGREDIENTS

Serves 4

5 shallots or 1 red onion, sliced

3 garlic cloves, crushed

2.5cm/1in galangal, peeled and sliced

1–2 fresh red chillies, seeded and sliced

25g/1oz/¼ cup raw peanuts

1cm/½in cube shrimp paste, prepared

1.2 litres/2 pints/5 cups Vegetable Stock

50–75g/2–3oz/½–¾ cup salted peanuts, lightly crushed

15–30ml/1–2 tbsp dark brown sugar

5ml/1 tsp tamarind pulp, soaked in 75ml/5 tbsp warm water for 15 minutes

salt

For the vegetables

1 christophine, thinly peeled, seeds removed, flesh finely sliced

115g/4 oz green beans, thinly sliced

50g/2 oz corn kernels (optional)

a handful of green leaves, such as watercress, rocket (arugula) or Chinese leaves (Chinese cabbage), finely shredded

1 fresh green chilli, seeded and sliced, to garnish

2 Pour in some of the stock to moisten and then pour this mixture into a pan or wok, adding the rest of the stock. Cook for 15 minutes with the crushed salted peanuts and sugar.

4 About 5 minutes before serving, add the christophine slices, beans and corn, if using, to the soup and cook fairly rapidly. At the last minute, add the green leaves and salt to taste.

5 Add the tamarind juice and adjust the seasoning. Serve immediately, garnished with slices of green chilli.

1 Grind the shallots or onion, garlic, galangal, chillies, raw peanuts and shrimp paste to a paste in a food processor, or using a mortar and pestle.

3 Strain the tamarind pulp, discarding the seeds, and reserve the juice.

Caribbean Vegetable Soup

This unusual vegetable soup is refreshing and filling.

INGREDIENTS

Serves 4

25g/1oz/2 tbsp butter or margarine

1 onion, chopped

1 garlic clove, crushed

2 carrots, sliced

1.5 litres/2½ pints/6¼ cups
   Vegetable Stock

2 bay leaves

2 fresh thyme sprigs

1 celery stick, finely chopped

2 green bananas, peeled and cut into
   4 pieces

175g/6 oz white yam or eddoe, peeled
   and cubed

25g/1oz/2 tbsp red lentils

1 christophine, peeled and chopped

25g/1oz/2 tbsp macaroni (optional)

salt and ground black pepper

chopped spring onions (scallions),
   to garnish

COOK'S TIP

Use other root vegetables or
potatoes if yam or eddoes are
not available. Add more stock if
you want a thinner soup.

1 Melt the butter or margarine
and cook the onion, garlic and
carrots for a few minutes, stirring
occasionally, until beginning to
soften. Add the stock, bay leaves
and thyme and bring to the boil.

2 Add the celery, green bananas,
white yam or eddoe, lentils,
christophine and macaroni, if
using. Season to taste with salt and
pepper and simmer for 25 minutes,
until all the vegetables are cooked.
Serve garnished with chopped
spring onions.

Chunky Vegetable Soups